I0160913

FROM CUBS TO JETS

Essays from a life in the air.

by

Joe Clark

© 2015 Joseph F. Clark
Saint Augustine, FL

All rights reserved. Except for fair use educational purposes and short excerpts for editorial reviews in journals, magazines, or web sites, no part of this book shall be reproduced, stored in a retrieval system, or transmitted by any means without the written permission of the publisher.

International Standard Book Number 13: 978-1-60452-074-3
International Standard Book Number 10: 1-60452-074-4
Library of Congress Control Number: 2014914349

BluewaterPress LLC
52 Tuscan Way Ste 202-309
Saint Augustine FL 32092
http://bluewaterpress.com

This book may be purchased online at -

http://www.bluewaterpress.com/cubs-jets

An Introduction

This book is for pilots. For old pilots no longer flying, for those who are training to be pilots, and for those would-be pilots who *dream of flying.*

In August 2010, I committed myself to writing a daily blog after my wife and I watched the movie, *Julie & Julia.* I am not a great fan of Julia Child, or for that matter, any other cookbook author.

I was intrigued when a blogger dedicated herself to cooking everything in one of Child's cookbooks and writing about it daily. It also made me realize I have been a lazy writer, one who should have finished my books long ago, and yet, still had not.

Moreover, here was a woman who had made a plan, set goals, executed, turned it into a book, and then with extremely good fortune, had the fantastic luck to have the book made into a major movie. I am sure the book you are now holding in your hands will never make it to the big screen.

The purpose of this book is to educate and entertain, no more, no less.

So, sitting on the couch with my wife, and with Gracie the cat between us, I explained writing a daily blog is something I had to do. "I have to write about aviation and writing everyday for the next year. Then I need to form it into a book," I told her—and the cat. Ardis didn't say much and the cat looked up as if to say, "Whatever."

With a couple of exceptions, I was successful. I only missed two days of writing. One was due to work, and the other was the day when my best friend's father passed.

There are four major sections to this book: General Aviation, Military Flying, Tips and Techniques, and Aviation History. The purpose behind writing *From Cubs to Jets* is to allow those who do not like to read on computer screens a way to read the blogs in book form. Some readers, including many friends, my wife, and myself, still like the feel of a real book in their hands. We have discovered there is something special in the pages of a book.

Most of the essays are short, with only a very few slightly longer. Readers can pick up the book, start reading anywhere, and skip around at their leisure. The only part of the book that could be considered temporal is the beginning, when I talk about my first flight lessons.

What follows are accounts of my first lessons, stories about general aviation, the joy of flight instructing, and my days flying in the U.S. Navy. For the student pilots and flight instructors, I have information about the technical side of flying, along with hints I hope will explain the mysteries of flying airplanes a little more in depth, making it easier to understand for those trying to believe in what is almost certainly magic.

The last section of the book is for those who enjoy history. In it, I reflect on some of the famous aviators, events, and aircraft that make up this wonderful world called aviation.

At one time, Benjamin Franklin said, *"If you would not be forgotten as soon as you are dead, either write something worth reading or do things worth writing."*

I could not agree with him more.

Joe Clark
July 2015
Saint Augustine, FL

Contents

Essays From General Aviation

Writings From Military Flying

Tips and Techniques

Essays From Aviation History

FROM CUBS TO JETS

Essays From General Aviation

"Airplane Smell"

My logbook starts early on a Saturday morning on the last day of July 1971, the year I graduated from high school. I had been driving around the country looking for an old man named Charlie Miller who lived and worked at his privately owned airport. The guys in the airplane propeller overhaul shop where I worked talked of Charlie with both respect and disdain. Those who liked him respected him; those who did not know him or disliked him, well, as always, you get the picture. Charlie is in many ways, responsible for me sitting here and writing these pages today. He was the one person who almost quite literally, launched me into my flying career.

Charlie's concept of teaching student pilots how to fly was tough and solid. I remember him talking of teaching the rudiments of flying first, not dealing with radios, control towers, and Air Traffic Control (ATC). After the student pilot knew how to fly, then he would introduce all that other "stuff." To Charlie, the idea of the student learning how to fly was the most important foundational skill the student needed to learn. Of course, Charlie believed the only way to teach pilots how to fly was with airplanes with tailwheels. And the finest airplane for this job, according to him, was the J-3 Cub. All these years later, I have to agree.

That first morning I met Charlie, I was 18-years-old and he was 71. It was a few minutes before eight in the morning when I drove up to his house. It seemed remotely abandoned. It was very quiet. The air was still and cool from the night before and I could easily hear the birds from across the fields, as well as the cattle farther away in the pastures. I felt intrusive on this scene as I got out of my mom's car and started looking around the hangars.

In the hangars, I found one of the J-3's I would later spend considerable time flying. I walked around the Cub looking her over from spinner to rudder. She seemed dainty and frail. This was the first time I had actually seen a Piper Cub up close. I could not believe this aerial contraption actually flew, much less carried two people aloft. After inspecting the airplane, I began to understand why the pilots of World War I referred to the first airplanes as "kites." Looking at this airplane built with similar construction techniques made me question how quickly the fabric might separate from the frame once the plane was in the air.

Placing my hand on the craft and feeling the fuselage while moving forward, I looked inside, marveling at the simplicity of the Cub's cockpit. When I stuck my head inside the airplane, for the first time in my life I became aware of an odor I would come to cherish forever: it was the smell of an airplane!

Now airplane smell, mind you, is something very different from new car smell. New car smell disappears after a short while, but the smell of an airplane becomes more pungent and pronounced with age. The scent of which I speak is a special odor, a smell of which all older airplane pilots are familiar. It is the scent of the leather seats with aviation gas mixed with the smell of the aircraft "dope" (the chemical) used in building the old airplanes of steel tube, wood, and fabric. It is a wonderful smell and there is no other smell like it in the world.

In the years since first meeting the old Cub, I have flown many airplanes. Some of the airplanes, like the Cub, were made of wood and fabric and smelled similar. I also learned these "kites" were stronger than most modern aircraft of today. I also discovered that new airplanes have little character, compared to the old airplanes.

And today's airplanes don't have that "real airplane" smell of those old taildraggers.

Technology

The technology we have today is amazing. Each day I grow older, I marvel at the new inventions, which someone seemingly perfected only yesterday, or maybe this morning, just so this evening will be ever so much more wonderful.

Often I tell my students I am too old, and I am too young. Sometimes, they look at me in confusion and wonder what in the world I am trying to say. I would have enjoyed being a part of The Greatest Generation; I think they had the most fun of all when it comes to flying, even though they got the shortest end of the stick regarding the world situation of the 1930s and early 1940s. I would also like to be young enough, or maybe sufficiently cognitive in my old age, to see the wonderful new gadgets the technologies of the future 50 years from now or so will bring to us. I always felt I was born too late, or too early. That's my story and I'm sticking with it.

In both my fields, writing and flying, the technological advancements over the last 40 years has been nothing short of amazing. In 1975, yes, 1975, one of the professors at the School of Journalism at the University of Florida, stood before us and said, "Newspapers are dead." This was not the thing to say to a bunch of aspiring news reporters.

He went on to say the news of the future would come to every household through a device. "Not quite a television set, but something similar," he said. Those of us in the classroom did not have kind things to say about this professor; many of us thought he was an idiot and wondered where he could have ever garnered such information. We knew the newspapers of America could not possibly die—they were the backbone of our news reporting system. Every intelligent person knew television reporting only gave an audience the broadest details of a news event. If one wanted to get to the heart of a story, the only way to get the full story was by way of a solidly written newspaper story, well penned by a real journalist.

In aviation, when I started training for my instrument rating, I flew airplanes woefully inadequate for instrument flight by today's standards. And I did my training "in the soup," in bad weather. In the clouds—where I could not see where I was going.

In those early days, our primary means of navigation included the VHF omnidirectional system, or VOR. Most training airplanes at the time only had one VOR receiver. This meant navigating along your course, momentarily switching frequency to another station, identifying that station, and then determining the radial you were crossing. Afterwards, you would go back to the primary frequency and continue along your way.

By the 1980s, many airplanes were equipped with high quality, redundant radios. Then we began to see other systems coming on line. Area navigation (RNAV) was brilliant! Distance measuring equipment (DME) was wonderful. Radios became more reliable and pilots did not have to rely on that 7700 for one minute, 7600 for the next 14, and fly the last of the "assigned, expected, or filed."

Now we have GPS—and almost every little kid and his or her grandmother knows it is Global Positioning System, or "GSP" as my mother-in-law refers to it. Not only is this technology amazing in the airplane, it is remarkable that we can take a portable unit to our cars and ask it where the nearest gas station might be, or the nearest movie theater—and it knows! Not only does it know what you are looking for, it has locations for almost any place you might need to navigate—in the entire United States!

How is this possible? And how did we ever live without these things before?

Thank goodness for the space program.

More Treasures of The Garage

First, it was the Dzus key, then the old high school yearbooks. Then we hit the mother lode. We found some very important old photos for which I had been searching for a long time. I shot these photos as a student in journalism school. They were B&W images of Charlie's place, the airport where I became a pilot.

I learned to fly in the summer of 1971. Charlie's Airport was a 2300-foot grass strip and he operated three Piper J-3 Cubs and a 1959 Cessna 150. He taught people how to fly in the Cubs and then prepared each student for his or her private pilot checkride in the 150. It was a wonderful way to learn how to fly.

Going through the photographs brought back so many memories. I had to laugh at the hairstyles and fashions of the 1970s. And as much as hairstyles and fashions have changed, the airplanes, the laws of aerodynamics and physics, and learning the basics of flying have not changed at all.

When Charlie taught us how to fly, we learned the rudiments of flying first, without worrying about talking on radios or using electronic navigation. We focused entirely on the art of flying. We would worry about radios and VOR navigation later; the focus was first learning how to be safe and skillful pilots.

N98048 on Final Approach

There was no schedule book at Charlie's airport. It was more like waiting for a haircut. There was a bench facing the landing area of Runway 9 and when a student arrived, he or she would take a place on the bench. Then they would wait their turn.

While waiting, we on the bench would analyze and learn from watching other student pilots land. Charlie would fly with each student only 30 minutes. At the end of one student's lesson, Charlie would taxi the airplane over near the bench and the student would climb out of the backseat. The next student in line on the bench would then climb into the vacated seat of the Cub. The "fresh" student and Charlie would taxi out to take off and the rest of us shifted one position down on the bench to continue waiting. Then we would carry on learning and analyzing, until it was our turn.

The Hangar

Occasionally, when the winds were calm, you could actually hear and understand Charlie teaching the student while on downwind at 700 feet. We could hear him because this was back in the "old" days when we did not protect our hearing well enough. We climbed into the airplane without any hearing protection at all; then we listened to the roar of the mighty 65-hp Continental engine and tried to understand what Charlie was saying over the engine noise. While it was bad for our hearing and difficult to understand what he was trying to tell us while flying, listening to Charlie from the ground also helped with our learning.

In addition to learning how to fly, we learned other things at Charlie's. If you were hanging around and it was too hot to sit on the bench or the wind was too tricky to fly, there was always a Cub in some state of rebuild to help with finishing. While rebuilding a Cub, this allowed us to learn about airplanes and how they worked. Working in the shop was a wonderful lesson covering many subjects; aeronautics, mechanical engineering, fabric work, engines, using tools, airframes, and getting along with others. This was a magnificent education, which turned out to be far more fun than any of us imagined at the time.

I wish I could go back there and carefully sand one of the wings one more time. And maybe fly 69 Hotel once more.

Joe's Luck

I was at the airport when a man inquired about flying lessons. He asked all the usual questions and then pointed to his wife and two boys. "Can you teach my wife how to fly also? You know, in case I have a heart attack or something while flying with them in the airplane."

I quickly think, *Uhmm, two students instead of one. Twice the flying, double the income.* "Yes, we can do that."

"OK, great. I would like her to go first." I thought that was a little odd, seeing as how he seemed to be the enthusiastic one of the two. *Whatever,* I thought, as I led her out to "Two Three Zero," a Cessna 150 I spent a lot of time flying at my first job.

I introduced her to the airplane by showing her the things we inspect before flying. I explained how we test the fuel for water and contaminants, check the oil level, and inspect the airplane's general condition. When we were at the engine, she looked at the cowling and saw the scars left over from an old sheet metal repair. "What caused this?" she asked. Being an honest flight instructor, I told her the truth.

"About five years ago, a student pilot on his very first solo had the number four (left, front) cylinder separate from the engine case. The airplane lost power, but he was able to turn downwind and make a safe landing."

"How often do you have engine problems in these little airplanes?" For a beginning pilot, I thought, it was a rather astute question.

"Ma'am," I began — in making one of the biggest mistakes of my life - "I have been flying for nine years and I have 2300 total hours and I have never had an engine problem." Never, ever, make such a dogmatic statement. Once it flies out of your mouth, you will not be able to grasp the words and return them to the depths of your mind and it, whatever it is you have just uttered, will happen.

Ten minutes later, we leveled off at 1700 feet over Tampa Bay. As I reduced the power to set cruise rpm, there was a very sudden and loud BANG! from up front. Power decreased a lot and the vibrations were terrible. I immediately turned back to the airport. The engine was only giving me 1700 to 1800 rpm at full throttle and it was a hot day. I maintained altitude as the airplane slowed down and I did what I could in the cockpit to restore power. I looked at my new student who was really enjoying her flight. She was, in a word, oblivious.

When the airspeed settled at five knots above stall, I could no longer afford to allow the airspeed to decay. While maintaining my margin of five knots, the airplane settled into a very slow drift-down from altitude at a rate of about 100 feet per minute (fpm). As fast as I could, I did the math in my head to determine if we had enough altitude to make the field.

It wasn't looking good.

On her very first lesson, I would have to tell my new student that in all likelihood, we were not going to make it back to the airport. Luckily, cow pastures surrounded us and when we reached 1000 feet, I made the decision for a safe landing in a pasture rather than trying to stretch it to the airport. Now all I had to do was brief my student on the upcoming off-airport landing.

"Uh, 'scuse me, but you're not gonna believe this," I began and then explained the situation. Her eyes tripled in size as she looked back at me. "Hey! You don't see me getting excited about this do you?" I said. Little did she know my heart rate had quadrupled about a millisecond after the BANG.

We were about three miles from the airport when I turned Two Three Zero into the wind on a northwesterly heading to line up with a pasture. I started checking for cows. We continued the descent with power and then something wonderful happened. The power available curve increased in the more dense air near the ground, touching the bottom of the power required curve. All it once, we were maintaining altitude at 300 feet above the ground. Since the terrain between the airport and our position consisted of pastures, I turned back toward the airport. We finished the flight with an uneventful landing on the same runway we had departed only 20 minutes earlier.

My two students continued to fly with me until I moved on to Part 135 charter work. I lost track of them and never found out if they finished their flight training through certification.

One thing is for certain: I will never forget them and the event of my first engine failure. And I will never again say something stupid like, "That never happens..." or "That won't happen..." or "That can't happen..."

Strawberry Fields Forever

OK, so I was bouncing about the web reading other blogs and came across FlyingGma's Blog. She wrote driving with her husband in their Corvette convertible to a fly-in with the top down. They started out on their motorcycle, but then changed their minds and took the Corvette instead. Then she made the point, "When you drive with the top down or on the motorcycle for that matter, you smell all the smells. The good with the bad."

It is amazing how the mind works. When I read that passage about smelling all the smells, I thought of two things from my past regarding "all the smells."

The first, involved a friend, a woman who had soloed airplanes. We were driving by a landfill and the road traversed from northeast to southwest. The dump was off to port (our left, south of the road). The windows were down and I made the comment, "I hope the winds are out of the northwest to keep the smell away from us."

She took a moment to lick her finger and stick it out the window at 65 mph. Then with her thumb, she indicated toward the back of the car and said, "It's blowing straight back." I damn near fell out of the car I was laughing so hard! It took me a very long time to regain my composure and then I had to re-explain the concept of relative wind to her. I don't believe she ever finished her private ticket.

The other memory was more pleasant. I remember spring and summer days when the strawberries were blooming. The strawberries filled the many of the farmers' fields where I flew ground reference maneuvers as a student pilot. And yes, all the way up to 1000 feet, you could smell the strawberries. Further south, over the orange groves, you could smell the orange blossoms. Especially when you were flying the Cubs with the doors open.

It was such a pleasant experience—flying the old Cubs over the strawberries and oranges. They smelled so good. Of course, there was little doubt as to what I would do if I had an engine failure. I knew in which field I would land. And then I would sit and wait for Charlie and the gang to come rescue the airplane.

And of course while I waited, I would eat my fill of strawberries.

The Cessna 170

The Cessna 170B

One of the best airplanes produced in the United States was the Cessna 170. Cessna manufactured 5174 copies of the model starting in 1948 until production ceased in mid-1956. The airplane came in three versions: the straight 170, the 170A, and the 170B.

The main differences between the three models include variations on the wing material, the wing itself, and the flap design. The first of the airplanes, the 170, had a wing built with a metal spar and ribs, and was covered by fabric. In 1950, Cessna began building the airplane with an all-metal wing, changing the model number from the 170 to the 170A.

The flap chord line on the 170 and the 170A is very small, making for an ineffectual flight control at best. Sometimes, pilots referred to the flaps as good for "procedural training only." Starting in 1952 with the introduction of the Cessna 170B, wing dihedral increased to three degrees and Cessna installed its trademark "barn door flaps" on the wing.

The 170 is a great, well-rounded all-purpose airplane. It has four seats, but as with many four-seat airplanes, it really is an airplane for three. Or a great family airplane for a mom and dad and a couple kids.

With a typical Continental C-145 or O-300 installed, the 170 is an economical aircraft. It delivers an honest 100 knots on 6.6 gallons per hour (gph) at 55 percent power at mid-level altitudes and in these days of high-priced fuel, this is a great benefit. The airplane holds 222 pounds of useable fuel (37 gallons) and squeezes out every bit of distance for each pound of 100 LL. With no wind and allowing for a one-hour fuel reserve of 6.6 gallons, the remaining 30.4 gallons allows the airplane and occupants a little more than 450 nautical miles in range.

In addition to the 222 pounds of fuel, a typical 170 can carry another 650 pounds of useful load. So, as stated above, it really is a three-place airplane. There is room and allowance for baggage, but again, this depends on the number and size of humans in the cabin.

Ground handling for the airplane is straightforward. Unlike other taildraggers, the engineers at Cessna did a wonderful job designing this taildragger. The 170 allows pilots to easily see over the nose, even while "three-pointed" on the ground. Other taildraggers must be S-turned in order to see straight ahead on a taxiway. This is not the case with the lower series of Cessna taildraggers. Not until you step up to the 190 or 195 do you have problems seeing outside the cockpit and down the taxiway.

As with all tailwheel airplanes, perfect alignment control of the longitudinal axis during takeoff and landings is critical. Let the airplane veer directionally, only slightly, and you could be in for the surprise of your life. The 170, as with all taildraggers, is an airplane you fly from the moment you leave the chocks until you return and shut down the engine.

For takeoffs, be cautious of a left to right crosswind. That wind, coupled with gyroscopic precession of the propeller when raising the tail is a recipe for disaster. To help, do not force the tail into the air; allow it to lift naturally on its own. When the airspeed reaches 55, ease the plane from the ground and let her fly away.

For landings, the best way is to three-point the aircraft. What many pilots fail to understand about "three-point landings" is this: when you come in and ease the stick or yoke all the way back for the landing, the moment the elevator hits the limit, the wing will stall. The engineers purposefully designed this characteristic into most tailwheel aircraft. Consequently, when the wing stalls, the airplane will no longer fly. If she starts bouncing a little, hold the stick full back and she will settle down and stop. If the landing is so bad and the bouncing scares you or rattles your back teeth, apply full power and go around.

If you ever have the chance to fly one of these magnificent airplanes, jump on it. If you get the opportunity to buy one, it will be the best thing you can ever do for your flying career.

The Cessna 172

The Cessna 172 was born literally right after the 170. There were a couple of Cessna 171s, but they were of no real consequence. During the latter part of the 170 production run, a couple of engineers and mechanics were goofing around and put a nose wheel on one of the 170s. They joked about it calling the airplane the "171" because it looked funny. The landing gear was long and the tail of the airplane stuck up very high in the air. With the round

The Cessna 172

tail of the Cessna 170, somehow the airplane just did not look right. However as bad as the airplane looked, the engineers, mechanics, and company pilots discovered something about this new "Cessna 171."

The nose-wheel Cessna 171 flew extremely well and easily. A short time later, the new airplane acquired a squaretail, shorter gear legs, and a new designation—the Cessna 172. After the introduction of the 172 in 1956, sales took off. By midyear, sales of the popular tricycle geared airplane completely outpaced sales of the 170. In June, Cessna officials decided to permanently kill the 170 line.

What Cessna achieved with the 172 is phenomenal. The 172 is the safest and easiest airplanes ever offered to the public. Indeed, Cessna promoted the airplane as being so safe, "anyone could fly." As of 2014, over the 58 years making up the life of the airplane, statistics bear out the truth of the 172 as being the safest airplane ever.

There are a couple of things that make the airplane so very safe. First, it is extremely easy to fly. Secondly, it flies slowly, on the low end of its performance envelope. Third, the airplane is extremely strong with maneuvering speeds actually designed faster than the aircraft's normal cruising speed. Essentially, a pilot has to work really hard to get hurt in the Cessna 172.

Since 1956, Cessna has produced over 43,000 units of the 172. When the airplane came out, approximate cost per unit was $8700. Today, a 2013 Cessna 172S costs more than $360,000. Much of the expense of the new model is attributable to the advanced avionics and glass panels of the Garmin G-1000 units installed in the airplanes.

Regardless of how the airplane is equipped, the 172 has always delivered sound performance and safety for the buck. For your operational dollar, you could find no safer or better an airplane than the 172. Additionally, she is a somewhat comfortable old airplane in which to enjoy an afternoon cross-country.

The Summer of '86

My birthday is in late spring and Paul's follows in the summer. I have known Paul since fifth grade, when we were in Mrs. Waterhouse's class at Alexander Elementary. Fifth grade was a long time ago. Right after we came to know one another, someone shot and killed the President of the United States.

Paul quickly became my best friend, even though I was a good Southern boy and he and his brothers and parents were from New York. They were... well... Yankees. To this day, I still consider Paul and his brothers my best friends.

One thing I liked about Paul right away was that he was very knowledgeable about airplanes. He was the one who introduced me to Alberto Santos-Dumont's Demoiselle. Santos-Dumont was an early aviation pioneer, a Brazilian aeronautical engineer and the Demoiselle was one of his earlier designs.

Had it not been for Paul, I may never have known about or fallen in love with the Demoiselle. Paul and I had big plans for building our own copy of the Demoiselle; the only things that stopped us were money, a place to build the craft, and a suitable engine.

Later, he introduced me to another great airplane and an aviator's way of life. The airplane was the Waco UPF-7 and the lifestyle was that of The Barnstormers, the original gypsy pilots, some of whom were very fond of the UPF-7. It was a great airplane for getting into and out of small fields while hopping passengers — $3 the ride! Guaranteed to be the ride of a lifetime! By the way, pilots pronounce Waco as "wock-o," not wack-o like someone acting foolishly, and not like "Way-co," a town in Texas.

Now, in the summer of '86, I have the chance to give us both a thrill. Aero Sport Inc., the FBO started by Colonel Ernie Moser and which was taken over by his son, Jim Moser, actually had an open-cockpit biplane available for rent, even if it was expensive at $75 an hour.

I decide I will qualify in the airplane and have Paul come up to visit on his birthday. We will take the airplane out for an hour or so as a treat. As far as I know, Paul has never had the chance to fly in an open-cockpit biplane.

His birthday arrives and we head out to SGJ to go flying. Open cockpit flying is one of the greatest joys anyone, pilot or non-pilot can enjoy. Until you have experienced it for yourself, you cannot truly comprehend what someone who has flown in an open-cockpit biplane is trying to tell you when they describe the experience. It is wonderful to go up and breathe air no one else has breathed. There is no finer sound than the wind singing through the struts and flying wires and drag wires of the wings.

Feeling the press of a 4g pull to the vertical for the start of a hammerhead turn is especially delightful, topped only by the sensation of the airplane stopping in mid-flight with her nose pointed straight up skyward, just before easing in rudder to start the turn to head earthward, straight down, as if to the center of the globe.

And as quickly as she lost airspeed going straight up, the biplane now starts screaming on the way back down. With the nose pointed right at the earth, it is alarming how quickly the airspeed builds, causing the wires and struts to vibrate and thrum and howl against the engine noise.

After we finish playing, I turn over the controls to Paul. He is content with touring the beach in the last light of the sunset. I am, too.

After the flight, we both know we can now check flying together in a biplane off our list. Years after this flight, another pilot who happens to be a movie actor would better put the concept into words. Morgan Freeman would star in the movie, "The Bucket List," with Jack Nicholson.

As we move further into the Twenty-first Century, we few who have enjoyed the "peculiarly sensual delight" of flying open-cockpit biplanes as Ernest K. Gann described flying biplanes, are a diminishing number. If you have the chance to "join the club," don't let the chance slip away.

It is possible that chance to fly open-cockpit biplanes just might disappear forever.

The Cessna 150

If you go to an airshow featuring Naval Aviators, you may see one or two of the experienced pilots walking around with patches on their flight jackets proclaiming, "1000 hours" or "2000 hours" in a particular aircraft. I came close with the A-4 Skyhawk, logging a little more than 750 hours.

The one airplane I did log more than 1000 hours in was the venerable Cessna 150. It is the only airplane I have logged that much time in and I must say, it is a fine airplane. Most Cessna 150s spent the majority of their lives in flight schools allowing student pilots to beat them up practicing landings. A few 150s were lucky enough to find homes with pilots who cherished and took care of them. Even then, they were flown to some degree in teaching people how to fly.

When the 150 came out in 1959, she had a straight tail like her bigger sister, the Cessna 172. Sporting a straight back fuselage without the wraparound rear window, the airplane flew faster than later models because of less form drag. With a 100-horsepower O-200 Continental engine, the little airplane would deliver an honest 100 miles per hour on 6 gallons of 80-octane fuel.

A 1959 Cessna 150

Most 150s weigh in at a little over 1100 pounds, giving the aircraft about 500 pounds or so of useful load. With 24.5 gallons of fuel, this typically left about 350 pounds for people and baggage.

Flying characteristics for the Cessna 150 were very honest. In teaching young pilots how to fly, the airplane was unmatched in the 1960s and '70s. Over the production life of the airplane, Cessna manufactured a little more than 20,000 units. Today, according to Trade-A-Plane, pilots can find good Cessna 150s on the used airplane market for prices ranging from $15,000 to a little over $35,000.

Dollar for dollar, it is hard to beat the Cessna 150 in terms of utility and fun flying. It is a good flying, safe, and economical airplane. A family could purchase a Cessna 150 and every one could learn how to fly in the airplane.

If the airplane cost $25,000, was stored in a hangar for $200 a month, and everyone in the family shared in operating costs to learn how to fly, the per hour operation costs could be held to less than $50 per hour. In today's high cost environment, that's a pretty good deal.

And everyone in the family would have fun taking care of and flying one of the littlest Cessnas.

A Very Pleasant Surprise

One wonderful thing about airplanes is that each has a lesson to teach. All a new or old pilot has to do to learn the lessons of an airplane is keep his or her eyes and ears open. The airplane will do the rest.

I was home on Christmas leave one year and went to the airport where I first worked as a flight instructor. When I walked into the office, I ran into a former student. He was dressed professionally and said he was selling airplanes. Good for him, I thought.

"What are you selling?" I asked.

"The Phantom II ultra-light," he quickly answered.

"Oh, OK," I responded. "Not really an airplane."

"Actually, it is an airplane. It is more airplane than ultra-light. They designed it to take more positive and negative g than most airplanes. You want to try it out? Got one all set up for demo flights," he said.

Visions of weight shift and warping wings came to mind and I said, "Naw, I don't do ultra-lights."

"You'll like this one," my former student replied. "If you pass this opportunity up, you will always regret it." Then he moved into the hard sell. He showed me the construction drawings and details, explained how the three axis controls operated, just as with any other airplane, and then he went over the weight numbers. He talked about the wing loading as well as power loading. My student said the airplane performed well in winds up to 20 knots. The more he talked, the more interested I became; turns out, he was quite a salesman. Almost two hours later, he convinced me to fly his demo model.

I told him I could not buy one, and he said, "That's all right. Take it around the patch a time or two. Go have fun with it."

So I did.

And I had fun, too.

Really..., a lot of fun. I mean, *a lot of fun.*

I flew a couple thousand hours off this little country grass airport. Every hour of dual instruction and every minute of charter flying was wonderful. I really enjoyed every second of personal pleasure flying. It was all fun.

But not nearly as much fun as the fun as I had with that "ultra-light."

When I lifted, I saw a couple of guys hunting dove near the end of the runway. They stopped and waved. I had seen them before from the cockpits of Cessnas and Pipers, but they never paid any attention to those airplanes.

I flew over a school bus spewing out students. All the kids became excited and pointed to the little airplane and me and started shouting and pointing at me and jumping up and down. They never did that when other "regular" airplanes flew over.

I took the littlest airplane around the patch twice. The takeoffs were shockingly short and the landings even shorter. The climb rate was phenomenal. In the air, she was a delight to fly. Feeling the wind on my face and tugging at my clothes reminded me of what flying was really supposed to be all about.

Yes, like all the other airplanes I had flown to date, the little ultra-light taught me a lesson. In her own way, she taught me not to be prejudicial. She reminded me of some old cliché about judging books by covers...

She not only reinforced the very important idea that flying is supposed to be fun, but that flying, which allows one to feel the wind against one's face, is especially delightful.

The Perfect Flying Season

The perfect flying season is here. Twice a year, the flight environment becomes perfect and those times are fall and spring. Fall more so than spring, but still, spring is good.

What makes fall and spring the perfect time to fly? It includes cool outside air temperatures, clear skies, and light winds. In the fall, during the time before the first blasts of cold frontal activity, the temperature is perfect for flying, for both the airplane and the crews. It is not too hot, not too cool. In other words, during the fall, the temperature is perfectly comfortable.

During the fall and spring, the skies can be crystalline clear without a cloud in the sky. In-flight visibility is phenomenal. There is something about the sky conditions during these seasons which seem to magnify the details of the land; checkpoints seem to stand out, and colors are vividly bright.

The winds are typically light during these times. It is the calm before the storm, so to speak. This is particularly true of flying conditions right at sunrise or just before and after sunset.

The best time to fly during the perfect flying season is at sunrise. I remember watching a Cessna 150 on the takeoff roll early in the morning right at dawn. It was a slightly humid early fall morning. As the Continental O-200 engine roared and swung the propeller, the prop grabbed all the air it could hold while trying to pull the airplane forward. In doing so, it compressed all the moisture out of the air leaving a contrail behind each propeller tip. Each trail spiraled all the way behind the 150 hanging in the humid air long after the airplane was gone. It was one of those moments I mentally had to photograph—because I did not have a camera with me at the time.

Another quality of the season making it perfect for flying is the stable air. Since it is not as hot as in the summer, the ground does not heat the adjacent air as rapidly as it does in July or August. As a result, in-flight turbulence begins later in the morning and dies off earlier in the afternoon.

Well, it is about time for the sun to rise. Excuse me, I need to go find a seat somewhere in a little airplane...

The Perfect Flying Machine

Every time an airplane makes the news, someone makes a comment about the "Piper Cub." Now the airplane might have been a Cessna 210, a Beechcraft A-36, or maybe even a King Air, but for many of the public, if the aircraft is smaller than a Boeing 700 series airliner, it is a "Piper Cub."

So many people are ignorant of the Piper Cub. The airplane is a wonderful machine that has trained hundreds of thousands of pilots how to fly over the decades since its inception. There is no way truly to tell, no one kept numbers the way we record statistics today.

The Piper Cub began life as the Taylor E-2 Cub in the early 1930s. Clarence Gilbert Taylor designed the E-2. Taylor was a self-educated aeronautical engineer from Nottingham, England. He and his brother, Gordon, formed the Taylor Brothers Aircraft

We don' nee' no stinkin' rhoonway

Corporation in Rochester, NY in 1926. When Gordon died in 1928 during the test flight of a new aircraft design, Clarence moved the company to Bradford, PA.

It was in Bradford that Taylor created his E-2 model. William T. Piper became one of the prominent investors in both the company and the new airplane. Once, when Taylor was ill and absent from the company, Piper directed one of the junior engineers to modify the E-2 in an attempt to make it more attractive and marketable. This led to a rift between Piper and Taylor resulting in Piper buying out Taylor, who then left the company. Afterwards, the E-2 became the J-2 and with further improvements, the airplane eventually became known worldwide as the J-3 Piper Cub.

The airplane was originally powered by a Continental A-40 engine, but other larger Continental engines soon replaced the smaller engine. The most common engine installed in the airplane was the Continental A-65 engine of 65 horsepower.

In all, Piper built almost 20,000 Cubs between 1938 and 1947. Because of the popularity of the aircraft, it is no wonder with such a high market share of training airplanes, most Americans believed all airplanes were Piper Cubs.

The Cub turned out to be the perfect training aircraft. The airplane was economical to operate, easy to fly, and easy to maintain. Spare parts were plentiful and the A-65 engine was the most popular light airplane engine of the era.

In flight, the airplane could fly at a top speed of almost 85 mph. With a cruise RPM setting of 2100, Piper J-3s cruised at a speed of 75 mph with a fuel flow of about 4.5 gallons per hour. While the airplane was not going anywhere fast, it had other traits making up for its lack of speed.

With a gross weight of 1220 pounds, the stall speed was less than 40 mph. This gave the airplane a very short takeoff and landing distance. Additionally, the airplane was incredibly forgiving; power-off and power-on stalls were very straightforward and the design of the airplane lends itself to very good stability.

The best thing about flying Piper Cubs is being able to fly with the left window slid completely down with the right window snapped in place underneath the wing with the door of the aircraft wide open.

Essentially, the Cub allows pilots and their passengers to truly enjoy flying the way it was meant to be enjoyed.

J-3 Cub takeoff

The Culver Cadet

Every pilot should try to fly as many different types of airplanes possible. One of the most unique airplanes I had the chance to fly was the Culver Cadet. Hubert, a friend of mine at the airport, owned one for the longest time. One day, he asked me to go flying with him.

What a treat; the airplane is a two-seat low-wing monoplane powered by a Continental C-85. With retractable landing gear and a small elliptical wing, the airplane scooted along at 135 mph. The elliptical wing possessed a total of 120 square feet of area, allowing for relatively high cruise speeds. This also is the reason for the higher stall speed of the airplane.

Because the stall is higher, takeoff and landing performance is somewhat lacking, along with climb performance. Once in the air, however, the airplane cruises very well, the main task for which the designer, Al Mooney, created the airplane.

Are you familiar with the name, Albert Mooney? Yes, it is the same Albert Mooney of Mooney aircraft fame. He is the designer whose specialty is squeezing out the last mph for every ounce of gasoline an aircraft engine burns.

Mooney and Knight K. Culver founded the Dart Manufacturing Corporation, which later became the Culver Aircraft Company in 1939. The company was active until 1946 and during the lifetime of the company, produced about 600 Cadet aircraft.

In addition to the Cadets, the company refined the airplane, developing it into a drone used by both the US Army Air Force and Navy for gunnery target drones. Culver Aircraft delivered more than 3000 of the PQ-8/TDC and PQ-14/TD2C drones to the military.

The Super Viking

One of my students made a derogatory comment about "plastic" airplanes when I mentioned airplanes of composite construction one day in class. He said something to the effect that "real airplanes are supposed to be made of metal." I thought to myself, *uhm... This guy needs a little more information.*

Then I thought of one day back in the late '70s.

We were sitting around the airport drinking coffee and hangar flying, the thing real pilots do while waiting for the next student, the next sortie, the next departure, the next mission. It was a nice morning and then we heard someone announce entering downwind for Runway 9 in a Bellanca Viking. Like all pilots at an airport who hear a different airplane about to land, we stepped out to watch how the Viking pilot would do landing on our short, grass runway.

He came down and greased it on. He backtaxied the runway to the FBO and we thought he would join us for coffee, but before he did, it became obvious he was an aircraft salesman.

We gathered around the Viking to ooh and aah it. It was definitely worth every ooh and aah. She was a brand new ship freshly constructed in Minnesota and she was, indeed, a true work of art. Compared to the other airplanes on the field, this airplane was a thoroughbred.

The airplane's lineage traces back to the first monoplane aircraft ever designed and built in the United States with an enclosed cabin. An Italian immigrant by the name of Giuseppe Mario Bellanca designed that airplane as he did this brand new Bellanca 17-30A Super Viking.

Giuseppe Bellanca

Bellanca came to the United States in 1911 with an engineering degree from the Politecnico di Milano University. He created the Bellanca Aircraft Company in 1927 and worked actively in the aviation field throughout his life.

Powered by a Continental IO-520 engine of 300 hp, the Super Viking cruises at 178 knots and can go for more than 1000 nautical miles (nm). A steel tube cage of 4130 chromoly with wood formers covered by fabric gives shape to the fuselage while wood makes up the construction of the wing. The landing gear is retractable and the appointments of the interior are the finest.

The Bellanca Viking

"A wood wing!" someone in the group says. "Is that safe?" Everyone can hear the derision dripping from his voice.

The demo pilot takes it in stride and then does something I have never seen done with a light airplane. He takes a run at the Viking, jumps in the air, spins around, and lands right on the wingtip. The airplane rocks a bit and then settles down and he continues his spiel from a comfortable sitting position—on the wingtip.

"I don't know if I would feel safe flying a 'canvas' airplane," says someone else. His voice, too, is filled with mockery and doubt.

The demo pilot slides off the wing, walks over to the baggage compartment and takes out a standard shot, one of those cannon balls which weighs 16 pounds that athletes use in adult field and track for shot put events. He steps away from the Viking, turns, and then hurls it at the side of the airplane.

The shot bounces off the fuselage and back at him, coming to rest at his feet. He picks it up, turns to face his audience offering the shot to anyone who will take it. Then he asks, "Any of you Cessna or Piper pilots want to try that with your airplane?"

Some of the others remain dubious, but I am sold. I will take a tube, wood, and fabric airplane any day over a "spam can."

Building Time

Today's young pilots face the same age-old, number one question as pilots of the last century: namely — how do I get a job?

Of course, as it was in the 20th Century, so it is in the 21st. New pilots find themselves caught in the exact Catch-22 as older pilots when they first started in the business. Many have pondered, I need experience to get a job, but I need a job to gain experience. This is the old classic chicken and egg conundrum. There is, however, another piece of the puzzle involving new regulations and insurance requirements.

Because of more restrictive insurance criteria, the first "stepping stone" flying jobs are now more difficult to obtain. Additionally, more young pilots having exposure to the more "interesting" aviation jobs are dissatisfied with the idea of working for a living. Some even believe they should have the right to fly jets for an air carrier the moment they finish their commercial checkride.

Projected pilot job growth between 2012 and 2018 is eight percent in the airline industry and 19 percent for other commercial pilot positions. Most young people dream of flying Boeing 700 series airliners and there is nothing wrong with this dream. However, they should not overlook the possibilities of finding great happiness in other fields of flying.

A new pilot with a freshly inked commercial pilot certificate sometimes feels overly important. Consequently, some of the new pilots may believe they are above working the menial jobs of aviation. They refuse to work what is probably the best, most important, and underpaid job in the business: flight instructing.

Flight instructing is a position offering great time building, but sometimes - little money. A flight instructor holds one of the most demanding and important positions in aviation and like teachers everywhere, they are not properly compensated for their services.

Two things about flight instructing are worth mentioning. The first is that new instructors learn more about flying than they teach their students. Secondly, teaching allows pilots to form life long bonds with their students and other aviators.

If a young person is not interested in flight instructing, there are other ways to build time for the airlines. They can become a charter pilot, but obtaining a charter pilot position may also prove difficult.

To act as the pilot in command of a Part 135 charter flight, you have to look at the regulations. Part 135 PIC requirements include a minimum of 1200 hours total flight time, which brings us back to the question of how to get the experience and therefore a job.

Other early flying jobs include sightseeing flights, banner towing, and flying skydivers. All of these positions the airlines will accept, but airline chief pilots are typically looking for more in the way of experience.

I often think back on one young pilot who was anticipating a career with United Airlines. After 4000 hours as a flight instructor, he became discouraged and gave his notice. He had no job prospects and no idea of what he was going to do. He did take some time to vacation with his family in Alaska.

While there, he inquired about bush flying. He found a position with an operator and gained experience in the Alaskan wilds. He learned the trade well enough and long story short, started his own operation. Before long, he was hiring other pilots and having the time of his life.

When the airline hiring boom started up again, he was told United was interested in him, his ship had come in. His reply? "Why would I want to take a pay cut, work longer hours, live in a crash pad, and have my schedule dictated to me?

"Besides, I wouldn't be able to fish salmon and hunt elk when I'm not flying."

If you are a young pilot looking for opportunity, don't close your eyes to things you think you may not enjoy.

What Makes a Cessna 172 So Safe?

OK, so I was checking out the stats on the blog and I came across this search term. Someone asked the question of Google or Bing or Yahoo, "What makes a Cessna 172 so safe?"

What a great question!

Here's the answer (at least my explanation and opinion).

First, the people at Cessna put together great products across their single engine line. When it comes to the 100-series Cessnas, I believe there are no safer airplanes on the market, new, used, or otherwise.

The first reason Cessna airplanes are so safe is the basic design of the airplane. Clyde Cessna built beefy airplanes. Later, after Clyde was gone, the beefy-airplane tradition continued.

For instance, one important distinction of the 1986 Cessna 172P (my favorite year and model of the 172) is the maneuvering speed. If you take the aircraft's Vgn diagram (a plot of g-forces against airspeed), you will find maneuvering speed at gross weight is 99 knots indicated airspeed (KIAS). Four hundred pounds lighter, maneuvering speed drops to 92 knots and then at 1600 pounds, maneuvering speed is 82 knots.

These speeds fall within the normal cruise capabilities of the aircraft. Another way to look at this: to bend the airplane and break it, you have to work really hard. Another reason the 172 is so safe is its ability to fly slow. The reason the 1986 P-model is my favorite is this low stalling speed. At a gross weight of 2400 pounds, the flaps-up stall speed is 44 knots; with the flaps full down, stall speed is only 33 knots. At lower weights, the airplane will stall even slower.

Why is this so important? In the event of an engine failure, a pilot can land the aircraft in minimal space. If needed, a pilot could even fly the airplane into a solid structure and walk away from it at such a low speed. This is particularly true for the pilot who can land with a 15 to 20 knot headwind component. With that kind of a wind and a stall speed of 33 knots, ground speed at touchdown will be phenomenally slow at 13 knots with a 20-knot wind and 18 knots with the lighter 15-knot wind.

Seriously, anyone can fly a 172 into a brick wall at 13 knots and walk away from it.

This one reason alone is why I am such a big fan of the single engine Cessna 100 series. Even their largest recip, the Cessna 210 Centurion is a great airplane in this manner. The Centurion is heavy for a single-engine airplane and is capable of cruising at 185 knots. With a generous wing area and high-lift flaps, pilots can land the 210 at 55.

Doing the Right Thing

I read an article published in a flying magazine that was one of the best articles written on the subject of flying. The article started with the observation of a cropduster landing to reload his hopper and then taking off again. The pilot impressed the author of the article by flying professionally and "doing the right thing."

The writer described how the old duster pilot did not waste any aspect of the flight; when he landed the big agplane, he landed exactly on a point to minimize his taxi to the tanks where he would fill his hopper. The magazine author was also impressed with the pilot's skill in both the landing and taxi in from the landing area, which the agpilot accomplished with very little use of brakes.

The author wanted his readers to get the message that the old cropduster pilot flew his airplane by the rules, as if he were flying a checkride—although no one was really observing. Except the writer—who, unknown to the pilot, was watching from afar.

Both the pilot and the writer impressed me. The pilot, for his skills as an aviator as described by the author and the writer, for his keen observations and talent at describing the pilot's competence.

It was a very good article. It is something I strive to teach each of my students today. Fly the airplane as if everyone is watching and judging, even if none one is around to see.

Doing the right thing also goes beyond the mere flying skills; doing the right thing includes following through with proper adherence to the regulations. Many pilots have great stick and rudder skills and unfortunately, must rely on those skills when their basic headwork fails them. This may place them in serious trouble, which may require extraordinary flying to rectify. When it comes to flying, not only must you have highly honed flying skills, you must always exercise good judgment.

If you fly with great skill and use good judgment, more than likely you will never find yourself in trouble. Additionally, your passengers will enjoy the ride and you will always have repeat business if you are in the business. If you are not in the business and only fly for fun, each of your family and friends will always be asking to ride again.

Another important aspect about flying right regards your equipment. If you are flying well, you are probably treating your equipment with the respect it is due. More than likely, when you most need your equipment to work, it will. An old pilot once said, "If you take care of the airplane, it'll take care of you."

There is one word that is perfect to describe everything in the few paragraphs above. We do not use this particular word enough; many professionals in various fields in addition to aviation often overlook or ignore this word.

The word?

Integrity.

Fly well out there—you never know who may be watching.

A Guy Named Joe

Here in Central Florida, there once was a guy named Joe. Joe was a fairly well known aviator, antiquer, and homebuilder. His day job was flying Lears and DH-125s for a bank; his passion was flying antiques and homebuilts.

Timing and geography were not quite right for us to become good friends. We remained good acquaintances throughout the time we occasionally bumped into one another. I believe we would have become great friends had we lived closer to one another.

I met Joe for the first time at the St. Pete-Clearwater International Airport. He and the fellow who flew with him for the bank, Woody, seemed to be at the FBO quite a bit when they were not flying.

I was always hanging around the FBO because like many, I started in aviation by pumping gas and washing airplanes. I was a typical "line boy" working at making ends meet while trying to break into the flying business.

I will always remember what I most liked about Joe and Woody. Unlike other prima donna corporate pilots, they treated everyone, even us lowly line boys, as real people. Whenever they were working on the company airplanes, they had time to answer questions. And both were a wealth of knowledge. They seemed to know everything about airplanes, aviation, pilots, and flying.

One day Joe showed up at the FBO in something different from the corporate jet. On this particular spring Saturday, he flew in at the controls of an antique Waco cabin biplane. This was when I discovered he was an avid antiquer. He had rebuilt the airplane and it was beautiful. You could tell every stitch in the fabric was lovingly tied and the fabric itself sanded and polished to the highest sheen.

This was when we started talking taildraggers and he became aware I had learned how to fly the old-fashioned way — in Piper Cubs. He became interested enough to ask more about where I learned how to fly and I appreciated his genuine interest.

I also became more interested in his projects. We talked about the airplanes he had flown, built, and restored. As I said, many knew of Joe in Central Florida for his exquisite work with antique and homebuilt airplanes.

After my stint at the FBO, I went back to college to finish my degree and started working as a journalist. My head was still stuck in the clouds, however, and I returned to Florida to complete my instrument, commercial, and flight instructor ratings. Then I started teaching full time at a small country airport near Tampa that had a single grass runway.

I thoroughly enjoyed what I was doing as a flight instructor. I would take my students flying throughout the region and on one flight, my student and I landed at Lakeland's Drane Field (see Old Airports, New Names, page 56).

While walking around the ramp to give my student a short break from flying, I was telling him about the different airplanes we came across. One of those was an antique 1929 Command-Aire biplane, of which I knew nothing. And there was Joe, working on it.

"Hey, you wanna go for a ride?" Joe asked. I looked at my student and asked if he was in a hurry to get back. He was my last student of the day, so I was open. He said he wouldn't miss this for the world and the next thing we knew, Joe gave us a safety briefing and fitted us into the wide front open cockpit.

I will always remember that flight because it was my very first in an open cockpit biplane. It was the same for my student, also. I will always remember Joe's graciousness and the way he looked when I turned around to look at him flying. Joe was back there enjoying the flight more than we were.

Thank you, Mr. Araldi.

What Makes a Good CFI?

Some believe you have to be a great pilot to be a good flight instructor. Others think you have to have great teaching skills. Then there are those who believe it all boils down to patience. For those who believe it is a matter of patience, sometimes they sell themselves short. Many have the idea they cannot work as a teacher of any subject because of their perceived lack of patience.

Somewhere in their past, they remember the frustration of trying to learn something or perfect a skill, perhaps one which they didn't quite "get." What they took away from the lesson was not the joy of learning and making small gains, but the memories of the frustration of their perceived failures.

But did they fail? Perhaps they keyed in on the anger of a poorly trained instructor or an instructor not happy with his or her position in life. Sometimes the frustration a student sees exhibited by their flight instructor has nothing to do with the progress of the student, but everything to do with the instructor's lack of his or her own professional progress.

Regardless of the reason, a student dealing with a flight instructor's stress is not getting the benefit of quality flight instruction. A flight instructor, who is working with such stress levels and passing that stress onto their student, is cheating the student.

And more importantly, the instructor is damaging his or her reputation as a professional pilot and instructor.

So, what actually makes a good CFI?

First, instructor have to be content with where they are in life. There is nothing wrong with using the instructor position to build time; most flight instructors are in the game for that very reason. However, while you are instructing, you have to give your very best to your students. While building time, you have to pass down all of your wisdom and all of the tricks of the trade you have learned from all those before you who taught you.

You cannot possibly pass it all down, but you have to do your best trying. You also have to do it in a cheerful manner. Remember the Law of Effect — your students will learn more from a pleasurable experience than otherwise.

If you are in good humor, you will provide your student with a pleasurable learning environment, one in which they can learn a great deal. On the other hand, if you are in a bad mood, the only thing your student will think about during the lesson is getting it finished and getting out of the airplane. Again, not good for your reputation as a professional flight instructor.

One reason some pilots think they are incapable of flight instructing is that they question their skills as a pilot. You don't have to be the world's greatest stick to be a really good flight instructor. As long as you are a competent commercial pilot, can perform the maneuvers and fly safely, it is a good bet you will be good as a flight instructor.

Conversely, if you really are the "ace of the base" and can fly anything with great skill and dexterity, it does not necessarily mean you can teach. I have flown with great pilots who could not teach their way out of a wet paper bag, and I have flown with some fantastic flight instructors who were mediocre pilots.

Here is, I think, the reason mediocre pilots become great flight instructors. Those are the pilots who have had to work hard at becoming a pilot. They are also the pilots who well remember how hard it was to learn some aspects about flying.

They never forgot what it was like when they were students, no matter what they go on to achieve later in their careers.

Why Fly?

Why fly? There are many motivating factors compelling anyone to fly. Each pilot has personal a reason as to why they fly. Some have verbalized their reasons, some not.

Some reasons for flying include a deep and resounding desire to soar like a bird. An older person may want to fly because it is something they have always wanted to do, but never had a chance earlier in life. Flying is a means of furthering and exercising your mind, regardless of age. It allows a young person to become more educated than his or her peers and it provides anyone a challenge to master.

One of the primary reasons people fly is for fun. It is wonderful to be able to look beyond the horizon, to feel the accelerations of the airplane, to go places and meet new friends.

There are many great activities you can enjoy through flying — adventures such as attending "fly-ins," or gatherings of like-minded pilots for the purpose of hangar flying and showing off their airplanes — owned, borrowed, or rented. A fly-in to a destination to meet with other aviators for lunch or just to talk about flying is a wonderful way to spend a Saturday.

Another reason for learning how to fly is using it as a means of transportation. For instance, a person who has a Cessna 172 at his or her disposal can live in Atlanta, GA and have a great weekend in Washington, DC. The flight to the DC area will take about four hours in the Cessna; in a car, the drive is 10 hours or more — in traffic.

The pilot wishing to spend a weekend at the Smithsonian can depart Atlanta after work and have a leisurely flight north, have dinner, check into a motel and be ready for a day of sightseeing first thing on Saturday. They can stay longer on Sunday, leave the area about 3 p.m. and arrive home by seven in the evening.

Those who have to drive do not have a chance to do a similar weekend. If they leave early from work and get on the road by one in the afternoon, they will be driving late into the night, perhaps past midnight. They will get up late Saturday morning, exhausted from the drive, see all the sights they can in one day, and then have to be on the road by 8 a.m. Sunday to make it home by the same time as their flying friends.

Travel by light airplane is a delight; it is a much more relaxing means of travel. When traveling by car, there is the constant stress of dealing with traffic, keeping the vehicle in the lane, and watching out for the dangerous driver that may pose a risk. Drivers also have to watch out for the constant monotony that might lull them into a hypnotic trance.

In the airplane, there is more time for sightseeing — it is actually a part of a type of navigation referred to as pilotage. You don't have to fight traffic on the roadways and the pilot, constantly using his or her mind to solve navigation problems while en route, can more easily avoid a zombie-like episode.

Essentially, an airplane makes a practical weekend out of a 500-mile trip. The same cannot be said for those who must drive.

Solo!

There is only one time, that time you get to fly an airplane alone for the first time. This is what it is like.

As I drove east, toward the airstrip, I thought of how little time remained before I had to leave for college. I watched the windshield wipers track back and forth knocking water away from the windshield and wondered how much more flying I could squeeze in before leaving for school. The rain seemed to get heavier as I continued east. I was beginning to think of the long drive back.

Passing through Plant City, the rain began to ease. Then the sky began to lighten just a little; maybe it was my imagination, but I believed it was improving. I was praying it would clear. The further I pressed on through town, the more I really believed the weather was breaking. I really wanted to fly this afternoon.

Reaching the County Line Road exit, the impossible happened: the clouds broke and sunshine came out and I could see some blue sky. The winds stopped blowing. The air became fresh with a freshness found only in Florida right after a summer thunderstorm. As I turned up Highway 92 toward Charlie's, I drank in that freshness and thought of the sky and what I would soon be doing up there in only a few more short moments.

I was not surprised when Charlie said he could only fly me in the pattern. The fact he said I would not be able to solo went in one ear and out the other. The only thing I wanted to do was perfect my landings, making each good and safe. I really didn't care about the weather, leaving the pattern, or soloing. I just wanted to practice landings and make them as close to perfect as possible.

We went to Charlie's newest and my favorite of all the Cubs, N6269H. I gave the airplane a quick preflight and when satisfied it would fly, I climbed into the back seat and strapped in. The old man stood at the front of the airplane and called, "Switch off!"

"Switch is off," I answered. He then began swinging the propeller back and forth. About every third or fourth swing, he pulled it through a complete cycle. From where I sat, I could hear the gurgling sound of fuel sucked into the intake of the carburetor. With a couple of more swings, Charlie positioned the propeller where he wanted it and called, "Contact!"

"Switch is hot!" I yelled back. I wanted him to know he was now handling a "live" prop—a prop that could take off an arm or leg, maybe end a life. With practiced ease, he gripped the face of the falling blade and pulled it through. The little Continental barked to life and chased away the post-thunderstorm stillness. Now, instead of the calm of the damp air, I felt the cool wind rushing past my cheek, pushed by the metal blades of the whirling prop creating an instant wind-chill factor.

As Charlie settled into the cramped front seat of the Cub, he told me to go ahead and fly in the pattern and to work on my landings. As I taxied out and completed the engine run-up, I noticed he seemed a little more quiet than usual.

Once I was certain the engine was warmed properly and ready for flight, I gave one last look around the pattern to check for other aircraft. Then I eased the throttle forward and moved out onto the grass strip. Pausing momentarily, I took a deep breath to relax and eased the throttle all the way forward.

As the airplane began to roll, the nose began to swing ever so slightly left. I countered with just a bit of right rudder to keep her straight and at the same time, eased forward on the stick to lift the tail off the ground. The noise, as usual, was deafening. The wind outside the open window of the Cub suddenly went from a strong breeze to hurricane force. The airspeed needle quivered over the "0" and then moved toward the "40" mark. As the airplane accelerated along the ground and through the air, the controls started feeling solid, to come alive! At 45 mph, I eased back on stick and the main tires became light on the ground. We bounced along the slight roughness of the pasture, and then lifted off! I was flying again and pleased.

Relaxing the back pressure on the stick, I allowed the airplane to accelerate to its climb speed of 55. Looking down, I saw the fence line at the end of the runway pass beneath us. I looked over at the school bus stop along Highway 92. Back to the left, I watched the smoke blowing east from the stacks at the plant just southwest of Charlie's airstrip. I noticed the airplane was climbing a little better than 300 feet per minute according to the vertical speed indicator. Charlie was still quiet, not saying a word. An unusual feat for him, for usually, you could actually hear the old man yelling at his students over the noise of the Continental, while you were sitting on the ground far below. At 400 feet, I lowered the left wing and began my crosswind turn.

I became engrossed in the mechanical aspects of flying and forgot all else. And of course, I was absolutely consumed by my happiness in flying on a day I originally thought I would be unable. Climbing out to the pattern altitude of 700 feet, I was again amazed with joy I found in the controls of the airplane as they bumped and vibrated and responded to my every input. The airplane seemed so alive! So much an extension of my body, my mind—I felt the Cub really was a part of me!

As I turned downwind, I eased the nose over slightly to maintain my 700-foot pattern altitude. At the same time, I pulled the power back until the tachometer settled on 2100 rpm. I always enjoyed pulling the power back as it eased the noise level in the cabin.

Looking down at the field, I made certain the airplane tracked parallel to the runway. When I was directly abeam the approach end of the runway, I reached forward beyond Charlie's seat, eased on the carburetor heat, and idled the engine.

As the power dropped off the 65 hp Continental, I let the nose fall through when the airspeed settled on 55. The next step was to trim the plane and control the glide until reaching the point of flare, finessing it until touchdown using pitch and skill, instead of power. Charlie taught us that way—to land without the crutch of throttle.

That was the real difference between pilots taught to fly by Charlie and others taught elsewhere. Everyone knew Charlie's pupils could successfully handle an airplane in any engine-out situation without having a serious accident. We were learning how to fly and survive at Charlie's long before we learned how to "sound good" on a radio.

Now my concern was making the best of this half-hour God had given me between thunderstorms. Around and around and around. More touch and goes followed by more touch and goes. Time seemed endless and the landings improved. I had no idea of time for I was unconcerned. All that mattered was getting my landings just as smooth as possible. I did not notice the sun lowering in the western sky, nor did I notice the weather moving further away. The sky was now gloriously clear. None of this I noticed as any pilot of merit would. It would be a long time before I was to hear and understand the term, "situational awareness."

I started to add power on about the fifth or sixth touch and go when the old man in the front seat pulled the power back to idle. He turned to me and said it was time. I looked at my watch and sure enough, we had been airborne the customary 30 minutes. Damn! It seemed as though we had just started!

As I taxied the little J-3 toward the hangars, I slowed down a little too much. Giving the power a slight nudge forward to maneuver toward 69H's hangar, Charlie gripped the throttle with his left hand and stopped me from going further. I had no idea why he would do that, as we were nowhere near the hangar; we were still out next to the runway.

"Well, what do you think?" he asked me over the chugging of the little Continental. "Do you think you could take this airplane around the pattern by yourself?"

Instinctively, I said yes. As I did, I wondered why my mouth said that. I was also acutely aware my body was turning to gelatin!

"What about the weather?" I asked.

"Don't worry about it. It's perfect," Charlie said as he got out of the airplane. "Now she is going to feel a little different and she'll fly a little better without my weight in here." He leaned in and adjusted the seatbelt of the seat he had just vacated—and had always occupied while I was flying. "She'll have a tendency to climb quicker and fly a little faster."

As he finished securing the belt, the old man looked at me and said, "You're on your own, now. Take it around once and bring it back to the hangar."

Charlie closed the door to the plane and suddenly I was fully aware I was alone. He stepped away. I put a little forward stick pressure on the controls and gave the engine a little throttle to swing the tail around. Then I headed back to the runway.

This was the day I had been waiting for all of my life and now I was scared! Scared beyond description! I was all too aware I had lost feeling in my legs. The taxi back to the end of Runway 27 was long, 2,300 feet worth of long to be exact.

As I taxied the airplane down the runway, I wondered if I would have enough strength left to run the rudders on takeoff. In my mind's eye, I saw all those headlines!

**STUDENT PILOT
CRASHES ON FIRST SOLO**

**STUDENT PILOT CRASHES
INTO PASTURE, KILLS COW
FREE HAMBURGERS FOR ALL**

**STUDENT PILOT LOST
ON FIRST SOLO,
LANDS IN CUBA**

I could also hear the broadcast media: "See it here first on News Channel 8 at 11!"

I knew aviators were supposed to be bold and brave. I believed I was born to be one and therefore had to possess all the same courage and bravado as others, as all aviators before me. Right? Yea! Maybe. Perhaps. . . Maybe not.

Then why was I frightened? And what was there to be afraid of? Hundreds of thousands, maybe even millions of pilots before me had soloed. Now it was my turn. As I taxied back along the runway, I wondered what had I gotten myself into. And I considered the outcome. But deep down, really deep down, somewhere in the cavernous, innermost reaches of my being, I knew. I really knew...

I knew I could do this!

The old man would not turn me loose if there were any doubt in his mind. Right?

I looked around one last time for other planes in the pattern and saw none. Then I brought the power up and swung the Cub out into the center of the grass runway. With a deep breath, I eased the throttle all the way forward, pushed forward on the stick, and applied some right rudder.

The Cub picked up speed and as it did, I held the stick forward bringing the tail off the ground. I noticed the feeling had suddenly returned to my legs. As the airspeed needle began bobbing on the lower limits of the dial, I looked forward and out to the right where Charlie was standing. There were a couple of other pilots standing with him, caught up in this, the most exciting moment of my life!

I could feel the Cub getting light on her wheels and noticed the airspeed indicator was passing 45 mph. I eased on a little more backstick pressure taking the load off the mains. A couple more moments went by and the tires eased off the earth. When the airspeed nudged 55, I brought the nose higher and we, the Cub and I, by ourselves for the first time, climbed into the late afternoon Florida skies.

It was magnificent!

For the first time in my life, I felt as though I was in control of my life. No one else had an input or a say or any other kind of influence over what was going to happen. It was going to be up to me. Me!

Alone! I was the only one who could now cast a vote as to whether or not I would live or die, land or crash, end life or begin living!

I looked down to the earth as the J-3 and I climbed into the sky. I could see Charlie standing next to the runway as I passed over his house and the hangars, and then over Wiggins Road. The western sky was magnificent! The sun shone through the humid air and reflected off the humidity and haze making a beautiful sunset!

I climbed higher into sky. I was frightened, I was scared, and I was excited! I could feel the beat of my heart over the sound of the Continental engine! For the first time in my life, I felt like I was really living!

While I was intensely conscious of living life, I also realized I was still thinking of the possible headlines that could appear on the front page of the *Tampa Tribune* and *Tampa Times* the next day. Man! That would be awful! But what the hell, I thought; and then I could actually remember reasoning that should I die on this flight, headlines on the front page of a newspaper would be my least concern!

Six Niner Hotel and I reached 700 feet and I looked down at the ground. Specifically, I looked at Charlie's little airstrip. It was a sight I had seen many times in the past four weeks and it looked comfortable and familiar. All at once, I became aware my breathing was again normal and things were okay.

Then I started laughing! I guess it was a nervous laugh, I was not really sure. Then I had the thought that, *Damn! I am really alone in this airplane!* The seat up front seemed incredibly empty and I could actually see the instrument panel and read the airspeed indicator for a change. This was a novel experience!

It almost seemed normal, to be flying alone. I arrived abeam the landing area and pulled on the carburetor heat, throttled the engine to idle, and allowed the airplane to slow. It was the same as all the times before when Charlie was sitting in the airplane. There was no difference. It was just another landing.

I looked down, flew a little beyond the cypress dome at the end of the runway, and turned base. Using the stick, I kept the airspeed pegged on 55 as I watched the runway. I was going to play the turn to final just right — I wanted the airplane to end up on the final approach course right on the extended center line.

As I turned final, I could see Charlie at the far end of the runway and I looked at the sky. I thought of the significance of the moment one more time and thought of what I had to do to finish with a safe landing.

The end of the runway came up and I could see the fence line. As the fence passed underneath the wheels of the Cub, I eased the stick back and began the flare. As the airplane slowed down, I kept it from landing by pulling more on the stick. At first, she wanted to climb, undoubtedly the difference between flying the airplane with Charlie in it instead of alone. I kept the airplane tracking down the runway and as the stick reached the full back position, I felt the wing sigh and enter the stall. Suddenly, the weight of the airplane left the wing and transferred to the wheels and we were rolling.

My solo was over.

I was thrilled! I was laughing, I was grinning, and I was happy! Even though many of my peers had soloed in nine hours or less, I was happy at nine and-a-half. At least I was not one of those horror stories I had heard in which students never seemed to get it. It was going to be later in my life after I was a flight instructor myself, that I came to realize this was no race; a student pilot soloed when ready. Not a moment before. Not a moment later. There was no race, no winners, and certainly no losers in this thing called learning to fly.

The airplane slowed to taxi speed and I looked up ahead at Charlie. He had already turned his back and was walking toward the hangar/shed/office/bar. He was done with me for the day and it was late. Time for a drink of his Kentucky bourbon. I saw him wave me in.

As I taxied toward the shed, I still could not get over the fact that I was up in an airplane all by myself! Yesterday was my mother's birthday. I felt as though she was not going to be pleased with this birthday present. I taxied to the shed where Charlie was standing. He was the only one around. The others had left. The little

Continental ticked over evenly at 500 rpm and after I stopped the airplane, I sat for a moment. Then I raised my hand and cut the mag switch to off. The engine whirled to a stop and the cylinders began making tinkling and crackling noises as the engine cooled down. It was very quiet and Charlie said something about congratulations and it was time for his drink now that he was done flying and oh yea, let's take care of your log.

The old man took my flight log and carefully scribed the words, "First supervised solo—OK." Then he logged 25 minutes of dual time and 5 minutes of solo time.

I looked at the log entry and for the first time, I felt as though I was really on my way to becoming a pilot. As with all pilots, this was a big event in my life, one I was certain to remember for the rest of my life. And I could tell that for Charlie, it was just another student solo. I wondered how many times with other students he had made the same entry into their logs.

On the drive home, the sun finished setting. It was glorious and a beautiful sunset. Then it got dark. Often, I think about that flight.

Now, after all these years, I also have other thoughts about my solo and of other student's solo flights. That thought is pretty predictable—one voiced many times by others. It is not truly accurate in the flying business—truly, not everyone can fly. But I have to think there is a ring of truth to that old cliché...

If I can do this, anyone can!

The Citabria

One of the finest airplanes produced is the Citabria, which spelled backward, is "Airbatic." That was one of the things this little two-place airplane specialized in—aerobatics—going upside down, turning loops, and flying Cuban Eights.

Champion Aircraft originally designed the plane as an offshoot of the Aeronca Champ after the company bought the rights to the

7AC series airplanes in 1954. Champion first offered the 7ECA Citabria to the public in 1964.

Originally powered by the Continental O-200 engine of 100 horsepower, the 115 horsepower Lycoming O-235 engine replaced the Continental engine within a year after introduction. This airplane was a tough little bird, although a little underpowered for serious aerobatics with either engine.

A year later, Champion introduced the 7GCAA and the 7GCBC. Champion offered both airplanes with the Lycoming O-320 engine of 150 horsepower. Additionally, buyers of the 7GCBC had the option of ordering the airplane with the larger 180 hp O-360. The original 7ECA was a perfect airplane for learning to fly or acquiring tailwheel training. The other two models are more appropriate for "working" the kind of work ranchers would do with airplanes.

In 1968, Champion introduced what I consider the best of the Citabria series—the 7KCAB. This airplane had a fuel-injected engine with inverted fuel and oil systems allowing for inverted flight for short periods.

The 7-series airplanes are very straightforward in flying characteristics. They typically weighed in near 1150 pounds empty with a useful load of about 500 pounds. Gross weight is 1650 pounds and with a wing area of 165 square feet, the airplane has a respectable wing loading of 10 pounds per square foot. The 150 horsepower engine provided a power loading of 11.0 pounds per horsepower.

The numbers above give the airplane respectable performance as a basic acrobatic trainer. She tops out over 120 knots and cruises respectably at 110 on a fuel flow of 8.0 gph. Initial climb rate is better than 1000 fpm. Typical stall speed is 44 knots and she handles well on concrete as well as grass runways.

As with all airplanes, there was always room for improvement. Refinements on the 7KCAB airframe led to the development of the 8KCAB Decathlon, which became a step up for acrobatic training and more suitable for competition.

If you have a chance to go play with one of these great planes, don't pass it up.

The Lost Promises

So, reveille sounds at 0530 this morning as it always does for me. Only I no longer hear the bugler or the voice over ship's loudspeakers, the 1MC, calling, "Reveille, reveille, reveille, all hands turn to..." After years of hearing the calls, I just wake up naturally now.

One morning after rousing awake a while back, I was going through various websites. I was on one website which is a great source of aviation news. A letter titled, "What Happened to the LSA Dream?" appeared in one of their features and columns.

Wow! Did this one ever hit home!

The author of the letter remembered, as do I, when industry leaders made promises: Flying airplanes for $30,000 and kits for $15,000. "A plane in every garage!"

This is just not the way real life is in the Light Sport industry. Again, as with almost every facet of our lives, the insurance industry created a great deal of problems. At least, many industry leaders report this as the main problem as to why their new LSA airplanes cost $80,000 and more. And there is research available to bear the truth in light of what is happening to the Big Three—Beech, Cessna, and Piper.

Product liability is out of control in this country. Frivolous lawsuits must stop—they are destroying the American Dream. Wait! Let's rephrase that; the uncalled for lawsuits are quickly destroying the American way of life.

Back when I was a student pilot in the early 1970s, I flew all over the southern half of Florida. Somewhere in the garage, I have an old Miami sectional from 1972 that has all my training cross-countries planned out. On that chart are dozens of little grass airstrips—near 100 Mom and Pop flying schools and FBOs.

Today, literally only one or two remain.

This is not an exaggeration. Increasing insurance premiums and the threat of unjust lawsuits closed almost all of those easy access general aviation airports. Now the industry has forced those of us who would rather operate off grass runways onto concrete, asphalt, or some other hard surface runways to which we would prefer not to expose our tires.

In the meantime, most pilots would not know what to do with an airplane that had to operate off a grass surface.

The Smell of Sunshine

To me, traveling from one point precisely to another is fascinating. Navigation is easy to understand when traveling on the surface of the earth. It is a simple matter of following directions. In other words, you can travel down Highway 92 for 3.8 miles, see the library on the right hand side of the road, turn left at that intersection, and find your way anywhere on the ground in this manner.

Navigation at sea, however, is different. There are no checkpoints on the open ocean with which to check your course. A similar situation exists in the sky. At least in my mind it did, until I learned about the process of going from point A to point B.

In the beginning, learning how to navigate in the air seemed confusing and difficult. I quickly discovered, however, it was not. Like many things in life, you just have to be careful in your planning and then follow through with your plan.

I soon learned about the compass rose, how to determine direction, and how to measure distance. After drawing a line on the chart, it is no more complicated than putting the airplane on a heading and following the line along the ground.

Sure, it can be a little more complex in reality, but not too terribly so. These are the basics. Today, many new student pilots are so dependent on GPS they are incapable of finding their way around when the technology fails. Back in the early 1970s, GPS was not around and the airplanes I learned to fly in lacked electrical systems anyway. In other words, if you were unable to draw a line on a chart, set a heading, hold airspeed, and identify your checkpoints, more than likely you were going to become lost. The funny thing about student pilots is that they rarely become lost; they only get lost after becoming certificated private pilots and growing a little too complacent.

With 2,100 RPM set on the engine, the Piper Cub flew at a blazing speed of 75 mph. For training, Charlie had a short route that took his students from his airport to Lake Wales and then to the small town of Fort Meade. The trip was 68 miles and took one hour in the Cub. We typically flew the route at 1,200 feet above the ground. This gave us a splendid opportunity to really go sightseeing.

Charlie would take us out one time along each route, the short one, and then the longer. When he was convinced we could find our way around the area, we would fly the routes solo. On the dual flights with Charlie, we flew with the doors of the Cub closed. Once I was on my own, however, I flew the entire route with the window and door open.

The first time I took off on the short route to Lake Wales, the path took me overhead The Lakeland Airport. Today the airport is known as Linder Regional. I prefer the old name, Drane Field. During World War II, many young pilots trained on heavy bombers at Drane Field. As I climb into the morning sky, I think about those skies of so many years ago. Those boys, who were 19- or 20-years-old in 1942, are now old men. Today, they are dying at an alarming rate. What they did during their time in the military was perhaps the noblest service of the century.

I think about those young guys as I fly over Drane Field. I look down at the airport, which is now a civilian field. It still bears the markings of a military base. I can see the circular parking spots, or revetments, where they parked the big bombers. I can also see the old ammunition storage bunkers.

In 1972, I trained in the same sky in which those young men flew 30 years ago, a time now some 70 years ago today in 2014. My flying on that day was strictly for fun. I have always sensed the debt I owe those brave aviators of so long ago. I wish there were a way I could let them know I do, in fact, appreciate everything they did and all they suffered through so that I could enjoy all my days.

Flying beyond Drane Field, I come across a woman in the country hanging out her clothes. I feel like a voyeur; her back yard is fairly enclosed, and yet, I still catch her hanging out her laundry. This does not happen these days; nowadays, we wash our clothes and they go through the dryer.

I miss the smell of sunshine in my clothes.

Unbridled Student Excitement for Flying

Nothing is better than sitting in the office and having a student stop by to talk about flying his or her first aerobatic flight. When the student becomes so excited they have a hard time containing their enthusiasm, it really is an amazing thing to see. That's what happened today. There I was thinking about all I had to do during my office hours, when one of my students dropped by before class to tell me of his experience at Sun 'n Fun.

He was in the right place, at the right time, doing all right things, had the proper credentials, when a well-known air show pilot offered him and some other young aviators the rides of their lives. At first, one lucky person would get the ride in the aerobatic mount while the others were to ride in a Beechcraft Bonanza flying in formation.

As my student explained, the pilots told him there was good news and bad news, and asked which he preferred to hear first. "Okay, what's the bad?" replied my student.

"Well, you are not going to fly in the Bonanza because it is down for an electrical problem," they told him. "Instead, you are going to ride in that." His guide said pointed to the air show airplane.

My student, a combat veteran of the Middle East, is in school working on a commission in the Air Force. He would like to return to the Air Force to compete for a seat flying the F-16 Fighting Falcon. The ride Sunday afternoon after Sun 'n Fun could not have been more appropriate for this young man.

Standing in my office telling me about what great fun he had while pulling 6g and slow rolling and going vertical, left me with a little doubt he would make a fine Falcon pilot. I could see into his future and knew he had a lot of school and training ahead of him to become operational in F-16s. I also sensed he would thoroughly enjoy every small morsel of his training.

We talked a little more about aerobatic flying, tailwheel flying, and flying in the military. I know he is on his way to having the time of his life. As I watched and listened, I wondered if I was as excited as he when I was 24.

I thought back across the years to the time I was about his age. I thought about the first time someone took me in an airplane and turned me upside down. Was I that excited?

I think, *Yes, yes I was*. I also believe talking with and teaching these new young pilots is what keeps me connected to my own youth.

For this, I remain eternally grateful to all of my students.

Flying the Ercoupe with Maurice

Down at the airport where I first worked as a flight instructor, my friend Maurice kept trying to get me to fly in his Ercoupe. For pilots unfamiliar with the Ercoupe, it is a lovely little airplane powered by an 85 hp Continental. It is of low wing design, with a bubble canopy and twin tails. The engineers intentionally designed the craft without rudder pedals and limited elevator travel. The idea was to design a spin-proof airplane. As I joke, I have flown an Ercoupe three times in my life: the first time, the last time, and the only time.

Actually, that's not true. I would fly the airplane again, but only on perfectly calm days.

My friend, Maurice, bought and sold airplanes on the side. I don't know what he did full-time, but he would always have an airplane or two up for sale. One day, he acquired this little Ercoupe and as with all airplanes I had never flown, once I saw it, I wanted to try it out.

Maurice was a good sport and willing to let me have a go at the Ercoupe, but with good weather, students kept filling my schedule. Finally, one day the students gave me a break and I looked at Maurice and said, "Okay, let's go take her around the patch a time or two."

Maurice looked at the windsock and said, "No."

I was a little befuddled. There was only a slight wind right down the runway. "What's wrong with today?" I asked.

"Not enough wind," Maurice said.

"What do you mean, 'not enough wind,'" I questioned.

"Oh, we have to have wind to fly the airplane," he said. "Got to have at least 12 knots." I walked away scratching my head. Maybe Maurice was getting a little daft in his later years. So, while we watched the limp windsock, we talked of airplanes and flying and tailwheels and Cubs. Maurice, like most older pilots, had learned to fly in tailwheel airplanes.

Talking with Maurice was always pleasurable. He was always good for saying something out of the norm. He was very well read on many subjects. One day, he came into the FBO and said, "I finally finished reading it again."

"What?" I asked.

"The Bible. Second time from front to back. Finished it nine months this time." As I started out the door to fly with my student, I wondered where he found all the time he had to do everything he did.

One day, I had to cancel a student. The student was in the beginning of his flight training and the crosswinds were too much for him at his stage. Suddenly, Maurice burst through the door of the FBO and said, "Com'n! It's time!"

"Time for what?" I asked.

"Time to fly the Ercoupe!" Maurice was like a madman. He grabbed a half cup of coffee, slugged it down, and yelled, "Let's go!"

I must admit, I had never seen Maurice like this. It was almost comical. He wanted to get out in the Ercoupe and said we had to hurry before the wind died. After a quick preflight, we were at the end of the runway. In a short time, we were airborne and turning downwind. Maurice was almost giddy with excitement. Soon, I turned the little airplane on final.

It was then I learned why Maurice was so excited about letting me fly the Ercoupe. I was flying in a crosswind. In a fairly strong crosswind.

I was doing my best at slipping the airplane to align it with the landing area. I was pushing with all my might on the…

Wait! There were no rudder pedals!

I turned the wheel into the wind and pushed on the floorboards with all my might where there should have been rudder pedals — but not. The result left me S-turning all along on final. I looked over at Maurice; his silver hair was flying in the relative wind of the open cockpit and he was cackling!

He was laughing loudly! At me!

We went around the patch three times and each time, it seemed as difficult as the last. And Maurice seemed to laugh harder with each approach, each landing.

When we finished, I asked what that was all about.

With a sly grin, he said, "There's nothing funnier than watching a tailwheel pilot fly an Ercoupe for the first time in a hard crosswind." Looking back on it from all these years, he was right — it was funny.

Thanks, Maurice, for one of my most memorable flying lessons.

The Just Aircraft Highlander

I saw a new plane at the Sun 'n Fun fly-in. This event includes seeing the latest designs from the creative minds of backyard and professional aeronautical engineers and technicians. One of the most impressive airplanes this year was the Just Aircraft Highlander.

This is a Light Sport Aircraft reminiscent of airplanes used in the bush. Equipped with tundra tires, a Rotax 912ULS 100-hp or a Jabiru 3300 120-hp engine, and two seats side by side, this airplane performs impressively.

Constructed conventionally using 4130 chromoly steel tubing, wood formers, and fabric, the airplane weighs in empty between 600 to 650 pounds. It has a gross weight of 1320 pounds per the

LSA rules. With a 100 hp engine, the airplane has a cruise speed of 96 knots (110 mph) and stalls at 24 knots (27 mph) with full flaps.

The power and light operating weight, coupled with 121 square foot of wing area, allows the aircraft to take off and land with a ground roll of only 300 feet. The Highlander also has an impressive 880 feet per minute initial climb rate.

One nice feature designed into the aircraft is the folding wing. An aircraft owner can trailer the airplane home for storage, rather than pay exorbitant hangar fees for storage.

Speaking of fees, the acquisition fee for the airplane falls into the moderate range. Some home built projects are much more expensive than the Highlander while others cost less. Regardless of price, when anyone completes building a Highlander, they will have an economical, fun, new airplane to enjoy.

For more information on the Highlander, check out the company's web site: www.justaircraft.com.

Uncle D's Swift

D was a different kind of pilot. (That was his name, by the way — just the letter D.) For one, he owned a Globe Temco Swift, powered by a 125-horse Continental. The Swift was a gorgeous airplane; she had tapered wings, a round tail, and pronounced dihedral. I will always remember D telling the story of how he had acquired The Swift.

It seems that D and his wife were on vacation traveling by car near an airport serving as a satellite to The Large Airport in the southeast. Apparently, an airline pilot purchased The Swift about four years before D ever set eyes on it. When D saw this airplane for the first time, he was northbound on his vacation with his wife. He got excited when he saw the airplane.

D is a tinkerer and a man of action. He became even more excited on his trip southbound when he saw the airplane sitting exactly where he saw it on his northbound trip. Oh, did I mention the airplane was crashed in a ditch next to the runway at the airport where he found it?

The airline pilot who previously bought the airplane had no tailwheel experience at all. But, as he told the onlookers, he was an ATP and "could fly anything." The old codgers with tailwheel experience said, "Y'all ought not do that." They advised him to take at least a few laps around the airport with an experienced tailwheel CFI. Oh, how pride goeth before the fall.

Of course, the new Swift owner groundlooped the Swift when he attempted his first take off. He was not hurt, other than his pride. He got out of the airplane, walked away, and abandoned her where she rested.

There the airplane sat for four years until D came along and rescued her.

I will never forget D telling the story of negotiating the deal, taking the wings off the plane, and putting her on a trailer to bring her home. For laughs and giggles, D pulled the bent prop off the engine and replaced it with a straight one. He pulled the engine through a few times by hand, rigged a makeshift gas can, and put a fresh battery in the fuselage. Then he climbed into the cockpit as it sat on the trailer.

"CLEAR!"

A few other aviators and mechanics had gathered around to watch the shenanigans. There was much laughter and shaking of heads. Most did not expect what happened next.

D pulled on the start cable engaging the starter motor. The propeller spun one blade, a second blade, and then burst to life! Then it settled on a nice even 600 rpm.

Everyone, including D, was surprised. What followed was years of reconstruction that turned The Swift back into one of the prettiest airplanes ever built.

Old Airports, New Names

We took my mother-in-law over to see her sister-in-law who has a winter residence in Haines City. On the way home, we took a route that brought us near the Lakeland Airport. I started thinking about the Lakeland and Orlando airports. Lakeland recently changed the name of their airport to Lakeland Linder Regional Airport. What a mouthful! To me, the airport will always be Drane Field.

As with many airports throughout Florida, the military constructed Drane Field in the early 1940s to train pilots for the war. Drane Field served as an auxiliary base to what was then known as MacDill Field, a place that later became MacDill Air Force Base.

Over in Orlando, the smaller of the two airports is Orlando Executive. Locals remember when the airport, located near downtown Orlando, carried the name Herndon Field.

Just south of Herndon, or Exec as some pilots now call it, is Orlando International. Orlando International once was a full-fledged air base known as McCoy Air Force Base. It served as a Strategic Air Command facility and was also one of the primary staging areas for the Cuban missile crisis.

To me, these airports will always be known in my heart by their previous names. They will always carry the old names, rather than the new.

1st Solo, + 40 Years

August 27, 2011, 1820 EDT

As I sit writing this, my mind goes back 40 years, almost to the second, of this instant. I cannot believe so much time has passed since the moment I first felt as though I was truly born. I was there, a witness and participant to my second physical birth on this planet.

Many will never understand what I mean by this, my second birth, into the world. Only those who, as I did, experienced this rebirth will ever fully understand. On the drive to dinner, my wife pegged it exactly: it was a life-defining moment.

Forty years ago at this very moment, I flew alone for the first time.

I have written about the experience before (page 37); it was a wonderful event. Now, all these years later, I reflect on the importance of the first time I spread my wings.

Had I not gone out on my own and learned to fly, I would have missed so much in my life. As my wife said, my flying defined my life and writing; it is, most certainly, what has brought me to this juncture, to write about this important event of 40 years ago.

I was, as I have said in the past, lucky. Luck, providence, and the fact the Lord looks out for children and drunks is the only reason I am writing this today. (I was too young for drinking at the time...)

Both the good and the bad peppered the road I have taken over the last four decades. I have seen things "land lubbers" will never see. Sunsets and sunrises reserved only for aviators and sailors. Lakes and rivers, seas and oceans from high above, as well as from only a few feet above the wave tops.

Because I flew, I was able to go places I never dreamed of until I saw them. And I saw places of which no one has ever before dreamed.

A pilot's logbook is a document filled with details of the pilot's life aloft. It makes for very dull reading. There is little to keep one's attention in the minutiae of a flyer's log. In reality, my life was never mundane, unless I allowed it. Most of the time I was having fun beyond description.

While my physical logbooks, like the logs of any pilot might be dull reading, my mental logbook of memories is fascinating. The challenge now, of course, is to write about it.

Beryl Markham, an English writer-pilot-adventurer who wrote *West With the Night*, opened her book with a comment about "her pound of papers and scraps" and such, memories and proof of her life in the air. I, too, have my pounds of papers — proof of my own life in the sky.

While the papers, logbooks, and certificates are important in their own merit, they do not tell the stories. The stories are contained in the events, places, and most importantly — the people — who have become a part of my flying. In my mind's eye, I see a kaleidoscope of images, events, and people I would have never experienced — had I not flown.

Some of the memories are good, some, not quite so good. Still, all are a part of the experience. If you did not know cold, how can you know what hot is? It is the same with night and day; you must have darkness to see the light. Life is that way. You have to live through bad times to enjoy the good.

Here is a good one. After learning how to fly and going out solo, I remember one landing in particular which I consider to this day, my one and only perfect landing. I had all of 19 hours logged and as I approached the flare on this particular landing, I could hear the long grass tassels of the runway, in need of mowing, tickling and smacking the bottoms of the tires as I flared into the smoothest landing of my life. There was no transition from flying to rolling. It just — happened. One moment I was flying, the next I was rolling on the ground.

I have made plenty of good landings since, but never as perfect a landing as that one landing. To this day, I am still trying to make another landing to rival what I consider my only one perfect landing.

I also have had my share of bad landings, too. If you want to read about my worst landing, read "The Almost Did Club" on page 156. This one scared me and provided insightful lessons about flying. You should never fly tired; it might cause you to become an accident statistic.

Unfortunately in my career, some of my friends did end up as statistics. Fatal statistics. Each has left me with the most hollow of feelings. After each accident, I wondered why they were so unlucky while I was so very lucky. I am still here, still flying, still writing, and still enjoying life.

My friends, on the other hand, are now over there, on the other side. They know all the secrets to life and in my mind's eye, they will be forever young. Their hair will never go gray, they will never be overweight, they will never experience the wrinkling of their skin, or the touch of their grandchildren.

While their passing left me sad with open spaces in my heart, each made me a much safer pilot today. Because of that, their lives were not lived in vain or their passing meaningless. I have taken the lessons of their mistakes and studied them well — so as to not make the same errors. And I take those studies and my work very seriously, especially when it comes to passing those lessons to the youngest crop of pilots graduating into the industry today.

Regarding these new pilots, they seem so young. I look at some of the ensigns and j.g.'s flying in the Navy, and some of the first officers flying Boeings today, and I cannot believe they are old enough for the job! Then I think, *Was I that young, too, at one time?*

It is then I realize that yes, yes I was. Just like the new pilots of today, I was once a "young whipper-snapper" as my old flight instructor once called me. It is just hard to believe he called me that… 40 years ago…

It really was… just yesterday.

Airports & Cats

Jeff and I stand in front of the hangar. As we watch student pilots practice their approaches and landings, we revel in the wonderful evening. The weather is perfect for practicing landings — except for the westerly winds, which forces the pilots to land to the west, placing the sun directly in their eyes. All else is wonderful, the temperature, humidity, …the sunset itself.

It is good to be at the airport again. I spend too much time working — away from the people and places I really enjoy. As we stand talking, the airport cat comes over and does what cats do. He rubs up against me and I reach down and pat his head. I also think our cat, Gracie, is going to be one ticked off feline when she smells another cat on my pants leg.

As I was thinking about this, a Cessna flew overhead and it triggered a memory of a day from about 12 years ago. Jeff and I were shooting landings in the 170 when I tired and got out near the hangar. He taxied back for some more and I sat down to watch from the side of the taxiway.

I watched as Jeff deftly took off and flew away. It was late afternoon, right at sunset. It was a very pretty evening and peaceful. I could hear the throaty sound of the 170's Continental as it climbed into the sky. I always preferred the sound of Continentals to Lycomings; the Continentals were deeper and quieter compared to the whiny Lycs. The further they flew away, the more quiet it became.

I relished the peace. I liked the quiet.

As Jeff turned downwind for 11, I could barely hear the plane. Truly all was right with the world at the moment. As he came abeam my position, it forced me to turn around slightly to watch the plane.

That was when I saw him.

And he saw me.

No more than 50 feet away in the middle of the access taxiway, a bobcat sat preening himself.

Huh, I thought. *I hope he has just finished eating. Maybe he won't be so inclined to eat me.*

I was smart enough not to move. I watched him, he watched me. We both seemed content to let things remain the way they were. I had no inclination to scratch that cat behind his ears.

As Jeff kept flying, I continued to sit and watch—both the 170 and the bobcat. I don't remember how many more circuits Jeff completed, but when he finished up, I turned around to take a look at the bobcat one last time. He was gone and it was turning dark.

It was time to put the 170 away in the hangar.

Writings From Military Flying

Real Pilots

My wife took on the most daunting of all tasks: cleaning the garage. For me, there were risks involved. For instance, she might find photographs which could be incriminating, such as the one she found of me with my arm around that blonde. Oh, well...

While the possibility exists of her finding more impeaching evidence of my life before we married, there is also the pleasure in her going through my souvenirs. She really wants to throw out a lot of stuff and she will come to me with something which makes no sense to her, but when I see it, I grab it, turn it over my hands, remember great times, and say, "Ah..."

The latest mystical memento she brought from some box in the garage was my dzus key. I explain to her it was the way by which one could tell real airplane pilots from ordinary pilots.

I hold the dzus key and tell her how we used them. I give details about the T-28B Trojan I first flew in the Navy. The Trojan had multiple panels secured with dzus screws. We, who flew the Trojan, were issued dzus keys to help access the contents of these panels during our preflight inspections. "The T-34 Mentor pilots did not have dzus keys and we '28 pilots did."

"Can I throw it away?"

"No! This is very special," I explain. "We have to find a good place for this." Not the answer she was looking for, and I notice her eyes trying to roll back into her head as she leaves my office. She really wants to get rid of a lot of stuff.

But not my dzus key!

Holding the dzus key brings my mind back to the days at Whiting Field near Milton,

My Dzus Key

Florida. There was nothing better than being a brand new ensign learning how to fly the Navy way in a huge T-28B Trojan.

What a magnificent airplane!

The airplane grossed out at 8250 pounds with two crewmen and a full bag of gas. A Wright Cyclone engine, Model R1820-86, producing 1425 horsepower for takeoff or at military power, gave her the power to do almost anything in the sky. What a kick in the pants! The amazing thing about the engine is that it could blow through the entire 178-gallon fuel capacity in a little over one hour.

At altitude, fuel flow could be brought down to a manageable 40 gallons per hour giving the plane a decent range, cruise speed, and endurance numbers, if you wanted to fly cross-country. While the Trojan did well in cross-country flying, her forte was in maneuvering flight. For as large a plane as she was, she was nimble.

The aeronautical engineers designed the flight controls very well; they were perfectly balanced and relatively light throughout their range of motion as well as the aircraft's speed envelope. One thing I really enjoyed doing with the airplane was spins.

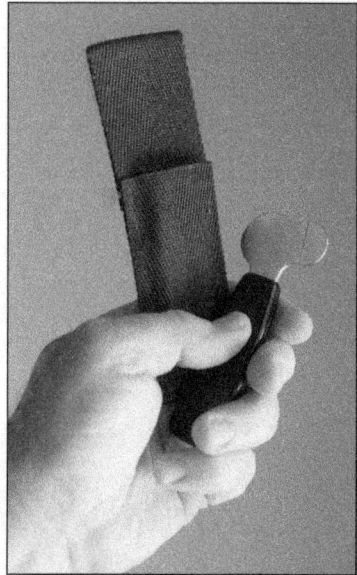

You would do your clearing turns, bring the nose up, and throttle back. Then, right at the stall break, feed in a bootful of rudder. The next thing you knew you would be over on your back with the nose falling through toward the ground. A moment later, she would stabilize in the upright position with the canopy bow just about at the horizon. When it came time to recover, full opposite rudder and forward stick would stop the rotation and break the stall and get you flying again in about half of a heart beat.

No, I could never throw away my dzus key. It is my talisman to the T-28B and the days I flew real airplanes.

Eastline Brief

Yesterday, my wife found my dzus key. After that, I found myself thinking more about the T-28B Trojan, the first Navy airplane I flew in flight training. Here is another memory I have from that time in my life.

There were five of us in my T-28 class. The day we started, a crusty Marine major sat us on a bench outside Eastline Brief. Another marine pilot, a captain, accompanied him. He was getting to know us and wanted more information. His first question was, "OK, which one of you sumbitches has flight time?" Immediately, I started sweating. I had over 3000 hours gained by my love of flying, teaching others how to fly, and flying checks on the night routes throughout the southeast. I was… well,… experienced.

I decided I wanted to get as much time in the '28 as possible, so I was not about to tell anyone of my previous flight time. I wanted no one to look at me and cut flights from my training syllabus just because I was already "seasoned." After all, I was not seasoned the Navy way. And I wanted to fly that '28.

I sat on one end of the bench and the major started at the other, going right to left. He looked at the first ensign and said, "Well?"

"I have about 20 hours, sir."

"OK. You're trainable. How about you?" he asked the next officer.

"I have about 200, sir."

"You might be a problem child. We're probably going to have to break some of your civilian bad habits." He looked at the third officer, a j.g., and asked, "And you?"

"I've got about two."

I noticed there was no 'sir' on the end of his reply. The j.g. must have been salty and knew more about how to play the game than the rest of us. The major looked a little irritated.

"What is that, mister? Two? Two hundred? Two thousand? What?" The j.g. clearly looked in his place now.

"Uh, two, sir. Only two hours." The major and the captain looked of each other, smiled, and shook their heads. The major turned his attention to the officer next to me.

"How many hours do you have?" he asked.

"I have a little over 15, sir. I just soloed."

"All right. We should be able to work with you."

The marine then looked at me. I started to really get nervous now. I didn't want to lie, but at the same time... "You?"

Right then I coughed and spurt out the word, "Three." At the same time, a '28 backfired on the line during an engine start. Everyone's attention turned to the '28, including the major's and the captain's. I did not get the condescending question he asked the other officer. In my mind, I could hear him asking, "Do you mean three? Or 300? Or 3000?"

But the question never came.

The marine and his assistant herded us up off the bench taking us inside to introduce the '28 training devices we would use to learn in our blind cockpit drills and emergency procedures. As we went through the door, I felt like I dodged a bullet.

I would find I would take that bullet about 10 weeks further into the program.

Vacuum Cleaners

My friend Mike commented he wanted to "see/hear" more A-7E stories. I read his email just before going to sleep last night, so of course, I was thinking of the days of the Corsair as I drifted off to sleep. As a result, I spent another night at sea...

Sometimes a night at sea is a good thing, sometimes not. Depending on how the weather is in my dreams, and the sea conditions, as well as my fuel state. If the weather is good, I am flying around during the day, the sea is calm, and my fuel state "above the ladder," it is a good time at sea. I have had those other nights at sea, however, when the deck was pitching, the weather bad, and gas was a question. Those are not good nights—in both my dreams as well as back in the days of real life.

We referred to the S-3 Viking affectionately and sometimes coldly, as "The Hoover," short for Hoover vacuum cleaner. This was because of the way the engines sounded. There was also a sinister side to the Viking and all the other jets onboard any carrier. Just like the Viking's unofficial moniker, every turning jet engine on a flight deck was a dangerous vacuum cleaner waiting to suck down any hapless crew walking by.

Late one afternoon, we were practicing for operations in The Gulf by preparing to launch a strike against southern California. It was going to be a great flight. My A-7 was loaded with six Mk 82 GP "slicks" and two Sidewinder missiles. Five hundred fifty rounds of high explosive incendiary (HEI) 20mm canon rounds completed my ordnance load. This was a mission everyone wanted to be a part of and we were all consuming a steady concoction of adrenaline and "can do."

I finished up with my cockpit duties and looked up to realize there was only one airman standing in front of my jet twirling his fingers. While that sounds like someone who is slacking, it was actually a very important part of his job. Typically, four to six airmen would stand around in front of the intake of a turning jet holding their hands up and twirling their fingers. This was the universal sign the engine they were standing watch over was a live jet engine. This warned others on the flight deck the intake area of the jet was dangerous. This was important because it was difficult to tell which engines were turning on a flight deck packed with 90 jets, some turning, some not.

I exchanged looks with my solitary airman. Both of us knew this was not a good situation and there should be others helping him keep my intake clear. As we were telepathically having this conversation, I looked to my right to see a senior chief walking down the line of other A-7s; he passes just in front of the intakes of each jet. If he continues on his present path, my jet will suck him into the engine.

I look at the airman in front of my jet. Then I look back to the senior chief. The airman looks at the senior chief also. We again have a telepathic conversation — we both know the senior chief is about to become grub for the TF-41 turning tens of thousands of rpm in the bowels of my jet. My left hand pushes the power control lever (PCL) outboard. I am primed to shut down the engine if the senior chief gets any closer. Both the airman and I know that if I shut down the jet, we will lose the mission. There's no way we can get the jet ready again in time for the launch.

I am about to yank the PCL aft to shut down when my airman, who is probably 19 years old, 6 foot 2, and about 220 pounds, breaks his position and tackles the short, 160 pound senior chief. They both go to the deck and the senior chief pops up first with clenched fists in a fighting stance ready to beat the hell out of the kid who just took him down.

My airman has an apprehensive look on his face. He starts twirling his fingers and moves back into position in front of my jet. The senior chief turns and looks up to the cockpit and we lock eyes. Suddenly he understands, looks a little sheepish, and raises his hands palms out in submission.

Then he lifts his hands and starts twirling his fingers while taking position alongside my solitary airman.

True Solitude

I have spent my fair share of flight time flying solo. In my Part 135 days, I was alone from Sunday night to Friday morning in the skies of the southeastern United States hauling bank checks to Atlanta, Miami, Pensacola, Jacksonville, Charleston, and other destinations. Each night, I typically crammed six to eight hours of flying into a 12 hour duty period.

All of my solo flights before or since pale in comparison to one flight I flew in the Navy. This particular flight is truly The Solo Flight of My Life.

The boat is about halfway between California and Hawaii. The mission is to go out and map all the surface contacts within 700 miles of the ship. The air plan calls for a launch about 45 minutes before sunset giving us an easy day catshot with a night trap. This promises a dying light on the western horizon which will help with spatial orientation on take off.

We brief and the air wing is ready to go. We suit up and man the airplanes. As a section (two aircraft flying together in formation), we are assigned different sectors around the ship to patrol.

As it comes closer to launch time, things start happening quickly on the flight deck. As pilots finish their pre-taxi checks, each calls up and ready. As I listen on the frequency, an odd thing happens. The Tomcats go down. Unless we make changes very quickly, we will not be able to cover all the sectors around the ship.

The next thing I know, my lead pilot calls me on the tactical frequency and splits the flight. He tells me to cover our original area to the north; he will take the sector assigned to the Tomcats. I could not believe we were going to go out and fly "alone."

Before long, the yellow shirts are directing me to Cat 2. I rogered the weight board, and got ready. Shortly afterward, the force of the catapult shot presses my helmet back against the headrest and I am on my way north.

I climb to altitude and get away from the ship. I begin looking for surface contacts. As I drone north, I am in awe.

The sun is setting to the west and all around me, all I see is water. After a while, the ship is 400 miles behind me, Hawaii is 1000 miles to my left, and California 1000 miles to the right. This is the absolute definition of solitude.

I do not believe I have ever been so alone in my life. There is God, me, the sky, the sea, the A-7, and that wonderful TF-41 turbofan engine chugging away behind me. As long as the turbofan continues to turn, life is good. However, if it stops, I know I will probably have a full night in the open waters of the Pacific.

The TF-41 keeps turning and on the way back to the ship, I connect with the tanker, taking on extra fuel. I spend minimal time in marshal prior to my push time and before I know it, I am back aboard.

After all these years, occasionally, I will dream of this particular flight. Only, now I know I will never again experience such incredible solitude as on that one flight alone over the Pacific.

Passing Gas

A pilot spends his or her entire life avoiding other traffic (code for not hitting another airplane in mid-air). And then one day, he or she becomes a military pilot. The next thing you know, someone says, "Go up and hit the tanker."

In radio parlance, Navy pilots call this "Texaco" and to be honest, it really is quite amazing. After finding the tanker and getting plugged in, it is truly great to be flying along watching the gas gauge go up. You can literally fly forever and never come down.

What a wonderful thought...

Before being able to enjoy increasing gas quantities, there is the little problem of finding the tanker and "getting aboard." After that, the next thing to do is "get into the basket." Then, it is merely the task of holding your jet in the proper position to put the correct pressure on the hose to assure fuel transfer. What could be simpler?

Tanking off a KS-3 Viking

Well, a lot of things to tell the truth. Especially if the tanking evolution we're talking about takes place in the dark. At night. In the clouds. With turbulence. And lightning. Oh yeah, and the deck is pitching and rolling the way a 1970s waterbed would if Elvis Presley and Rodney Dangerfield were engaged in a serious wrestling match on top of it.

Yes, there are just a few little challenges involved in passing gas at altitude. The amazing thing about it is the apparent ease with which flight crews accomplish this feat daily and nightly.

The Army Air Services flew the first in-flight refueling mission on June 27, 1923. The team consisted of Army aviators Captain Lowell H. Smith, and Lieutenants John Richter, Virgil Hine and Frank Seifert. The aircraft were slow-moving DH-4B biplanes of the Army Air Services. Basically, the crew of the higher biplane passed a fuel hose to the lower aircraft and the gas flowed by gravity via the standard fueling port. This is probably why the Air Force still does it that way to this day; they plug into the receiver aircraft while in the Navy, the receiver plugs into "the basket" of the tanker.

June 27, 1923

While they had the concept as early as 1923, the military did not start real air-to-air refueling operations until after World War II. Korea was the first conflict in which aerial refueling played an important role, and by the time the Vietnam War rolled around, the military guys had the process well tamed. They also had the equipment refined to the point that for the most part, it was reliable—most of the time.

Unfortunately, it sometimes fails, or breaks, or a nervous pilot can incite a failure. Then it becomes a real challenge trying to either get the airplane down to the destination, or come up with an alternate plan involving a lot less fuel than on the tanking plan.

The key? Just be smooth, turn off your radar so you don't fry the tanker pilot, sit back, and relax. It's all good, and once you're in the basket, you can stay up there a long time.

-30-

Timing is Everything

Somewhere out at sea tonight, Navy pilots will finish up their mission briefs and then, just like in the movies, they will sync up their watches. What they are doing is synchronizing their wristwatches with the PLAT (pilot landing aid television). They do this because sometimes it is hard to tell which number the minute hand on the eight-day clock is pointing to in the cockpit. Looking at the digital wristwatch is much better for telling the exact time.

This is important for many reasons. If a pilot is going out to deliver weapons, typically the bombs must be on target at a specified time, +/- 7 seconds. And then, in order to return to the ship, pilots must go into a holding pattern called "marshal," which they must leave at a certain time, a "push time" if you will, and they must leave within five seconds of that precise moment. On leaving, they are required to set certain parameters on their jet and maintain a strict 250 knots on the way to the ship.

Timing and speed and flight discipline is important for the aerial choreography to work perfectly. For there is only one minute between aircraft; when the pilot in marshal at "Angels 14" (14,000 feet) "pushes," exactly one minute later, the pilot at Angels 15 departs marshal, flying the same profile.

It is an amazing thing to watch from the deck of the ship. It is a sight few civilians have had the privilege of witnessing. Looking aft on a clear night, you can see a string of navigation lights and speed indexers forming a perfect line approaching from the dark.

The airplanes, spaced exactly at one minute intervals, give the deck crew about 30 seconds to get one airplane "out of the wires" and prepare the flight deck for the arrival of the next. When the airplane hits and pulls the wire out the length of its travel, the pilot eases the throttle to full power. This is necessary in the event the hook skips over the wires or otherwise does not grab one. Should the airplane miss the wires, the pilot is at full power and ready for the go around, also known as a "bolter."

On the port side, near the aft of the flight deck, there is a platform populated by other pilots. These are the Landing Signal Officers (LSOs) who work very hard to keep the pilots in the planes as safe as possible while landing. The LSOs, also known as "Paddles" for a nickname earned from the days when they used visual paddles to bring airplanes aboard the ship, closely monitor each approaching aircraft. If the aircraft is out of parameters for a safe landing, the LSO will hit a switch activating the wave off lights. He holds the switch in his hand, high above his head, ready to pull the trigger if required.

In the cockpit, the pilots have one of the hardest jobs. They must fly instruments all the way down to about 200 feet and then transition to a visual landing. Many aboard the ship monitor each pilot's approach. The first are the radar controllers, watching the approach on their screens. When the aircraft is about half a mile behind the ship, the controller will say, "Three One Two, half a mile, call the ball."

That's the pilot's cue. His response is to look up, site the meatball on the Fresnel lens, and call out, "Three One Two, Hornet Ball, four point two." This transfers control to the LSOs coupled with telling the world how much gas remains, in this case, 4200 pounds.

"Roger, ball!" the LSO's response. Now the LSO is in control of monitoring the approach for safety and the pilot is sitting in the airplane reciting the Navy pilot's mantra, "Meatball, lineup, angle-of-attack. Meatball, lineup, angle-of-attack. Meatball, lineup, angle-of-attack."

The airplane responds smoothly to the careful and deft inputs of the pilot's hands on the stick and throttles, feet on the rudders. The pilot controls altitude by the throttles, speed by the angle-of-attack, and the line up with quick and perfect movements of stick and rudder.

As the aircraft approaches, if the pilot keeps the meatball perfectly centered, the aircraft lined up on the centerline of the landing area, and the aircraft "on speed," the hook will grab the number three wire, the third of four wires from the aft end of the ship. In less than 300 feet of distance, the airplane will come to a screeching halt. From faster than 134 knots (152 mph), the wires will snag the airplane out of the sky more rapidly than the catapult shot that slung her into flight.

Yeah, this evening, Navy pilots are going to be briefing and syncing their watches for their night missions. I wish I were with them—but maybe not.

Maybe if I were young again...

Sealord and the Atlantic

It is the day after Mother's Day and for her treat, I take my wife, Ardis, to dinner at the Reef Restaurant on the beach. As is always the case, whenever I look out to sea, my mind wanders back a couple of decades to the time I was learning how to fly Corsairs high above this very ocean.

"Sealord" was in control of all that happened in the oceanic skies. His was the disembodied voice inside my helmet who always answered when needed. As I raced around the sky, sometimes as fast as my A-7 could manage, I imagined Sealord sitting at his scope watching all the training battles rage.

One day the mission called for two of us new guys to work as a team against our instructor who was playing the role of the bad guy. The profile called for departing NAS Cecil with a running rendezvous with a climb in a cruise formation to FL 250 where the 2 v 1 Air Combat Maneuvering (ACM) would take place over the sea to the east.

As we came out of the chocks, I was the last one. Something was wrong with my jet, but fortunately, the final checkers were able to fix it. Because the other two jets were cooling their heels in marshal underneath the tower, the men working on my jet as final checkers were rushing.

I have always disliked rushing or hurrying for any reason. If someone is going to make a mistake, it will happen when they are in a hurry to finish a job. This is one of those universal rules that bites anyone and everyone who is in too much of a hurry. Now I found myself in that very situation.

As the final checkers were rushing around my jet to finish making certain everything was as it should be and the jet safe to fly, I was inside the jet rushing myself. I met with the other two in marshal and as I came around the corner, Lead called for taxi.

Soon we were on the runway. Lead was to the right, Dash 2 was on the centerline, and I was to the left for takeoff. Lead looked over his shoulder and gave the turn up signal and Dash 2 passed it on to me. I pushed my power lever up and checked my gauges; everything looked good and I turned and inspected Dash 2's jet. I saw no missing panels, no fluids coming out of his jet, he looked good. At the same time, he was checking out my jet.

I gave him the thumbs up, he turned and checked out Lead's jet and passed the thumbs up on. At that, Lead released his brakes, 10 seconds later, Dash 2 began his takeoff roll, and 10 seconds after that, I started down the runway. I watched as Dash 2 joined with Lead and a few moments later, I joined.

After checking in with Sealord, we set up for the engagements. I really enjoyed ACM. ACM was not as concrete as dropping bombs, but still, it was fun. The nice thing about dropping bombs is that it was very objective; you had spotters on the ground who could tell how well you were doing your job. You could walk into the O-Club at the end of the day and throw down your kneeboard card on which you had scribbled your record of hits for the mission.

ACM on the other hand, was much more subjective and prone to one pilot declaring a victory only to hear comments from his opponent proclaiming, "Naw! You were way out of range and about 10 degrees out of parameter. No way you could have got me!"

Yeah, bombs are better.

We wrapped up from the last engagement and Lead called the final knock-it-off of the day. Since I was the one closest to America, the other two jets joined on me. The other new guy joined on my right and the Lead came up on my left. I was just about to pass the lead to him when all of a sudden, I heard a mike button click and he said, "Uh-oh."

I hate it when someone says "uh-oh" while looking into my mouth, at my medical x-rays, under the hood of my car, or at my jet.

It turned out that in the final checkers' haste to get the job done, they only snapped two of the six latches that held the panel covering the avionics bay in place. This was normal procedure when the ordnancemen still had to arm the gun. However, since the problem caused the sailors to alter the final sequence, things got dropped. Since it was on the left side of the airplane and because I was to the left on the runway, no one had a chance to see the unfastened latches. Now the problem was the possibility of the panel falling off the airplane as I flew back to base over the city of Jacksonville.

I detached to fly "a hung ordinance approach" on my own back to Cecil. The other two proceeded on. I was confident the panel would stay on the airplane; after all, I had just spent 45 minutes ripping around the sky pulling four to five g's. The approach and landing were uneventful.

However, the flight left a bad taste in my mouth for being in a hurry — all the way to this day.

Extremes

I like the extremes, except when it comes to the cold. After the month of September, I cannot go north of Jacksonville. It is just too cold that far north.

I think my dislike of the cold stems from a couple of things prevalent in my life. I was born in the South and with few exceptions, I lived almost my entire life at lower latitudes. The other factor in my dislike of the cold occurred in the Pacific Ocean in August 1983.

We were undergoing deep water survival requalification and as part of the drill, we were dropped off one by one into the Pacific Ocean about two miles at sea west of Navy North Island in San Diego. We treaded water while waiting for an HC-46 from the station to pluck us out of the water.

Do you know how cold the Pacific Ocean water is in August? It was about 68 degrees Fahrenheit, which is really cold. Especially when you are stuck in it almost two hours.

I was the seventh man into the water and as I slowly drifted off to Mexico, I watched as the Sea Knight picked up the six pilots in front of me. By now, I had been in the water for about 30 minutes and all I wanted was for those guys in the helo to hoist me into the belly of the helo, get me out of the water, and somehow get me warm. At this point in the exercise, in my mind it was all about me.

I was so happy watching the helo lift the sixth man. I knew the Sea Knight pilots would soon come for me, the crewmen in the back would lower the hoist, and I would be out of the cold.

What happened in reality was the helo flew to me, the pilots looked at me, turned and flew away. I cursed everyone associated with helicopters for about three minutes as I watched the Sea Knight run for North Island. Later, after they returned to finally pull me out of the cold Pacific, the crew told me their load was getting too heavy and the helo needed to refuel. In the meantime, I think I nearly froze to death while waiting. Consequently, I cannot stand cold weather.

When it comes to altitudes, I like flying really low, and really high. Up at the high Flight Levels, one can almost see the curvature of the earth. The sky is dark blue, even in the brightest sunshine. You can really see a very long way from up there! And the air is so thin that you can really make time across the ground.

When flying that high in less dense air, the indicated airspeed is relatively low. However, the true airspeed is high and if you are lucky enough to hook up with a tailwind of sorts, especially associated with the jet stream, you can really make some significant speed over the ground.

Of course, even if you are clocking across the ground at about 700 miles per hour, it doesn't seem as though you are even moving. That's the disadvantage to flying so high. All you are doing up there is sitting in the cockpit watching the DME count down or up while watching the scenery slip slowly by.

The opposite to this is flying really, really, low and fast. In the attack community, we're talking 150 to 200 feet above the ground. Pushing 540 knots—nine nautical miles per minute. About 623 miles per hour. And then reaching the target with your load of bombs, popping, and hitting a the target.

Yeah, I like extremes… Well, except for the cold.

Any Attitude, Any Airspeed

I am sure you have heard old flight instructors or pilots say, "An airplane can stall in any attitude or any airspeed." Come on, admit it. You really didn't believe them did you? I mean, how is it possible for an airplane going straight down in vertical flight to stall?

It is rather hard to grasp the concept of the wing of an aircraft in a fully stalled condition with the nose pointed straight down at the earth and the throttle wide open. After all, when you learned how to fly slow flight and stalls, wasn't it amazing how quickly the airplane began flying when you lowered the nose just a little bit? So if a pilot had the nose pointed straight at the ground, the wing would have to be flying. Right?

Well, maybe not.

I have been that pilot. Had the nose of the aircraft pointed straight at the ground, had the throttle wide open, had 600 plus knots indicated, and had my wing completely stalled out.

My operations officer, another squadron pilot, and I were in a "fur-ball" against two Tomcats. The Tomcat crews had to get a check in the box for their 2 v 3 dogfight qualifications. As we finished the fight, my Ops O detached me from the formation to go out to find and fight a lone F-14, piloted by a first tour aviator, or "nugget."

All I had to go on was the fact that he was in the western operations area cruising eastbound at about 20,000 feet. I was up about 28,000 feet hawking the sky below for the lone Tomcat. We were both becoming fuel critical and would only have a chance to engage in limited DACM (dissimilar air combat maneuvering).

I obtained "visual" first and was anxious to get the fight going so when the pilot radioed, "Challenger, where are you?" I answered by telling him I was about three miles out at his one o'clock high. I could see him, but he could not see me, even with the guy in the back seat running radar.

He called again and I answered, "I am at your high two o'clock, two miles." I could not believe the two guys in the Tomcat could not see me. He called again for my position as I was approaching his three o'clock position. I told him again where I was. Now I was getting irritated and more anxious to get the fight going.

As I went by his wing line, I rolled my A-4 about 140 degrees starboard and put about 4.5 g's on the airplane. Using the altitude advantage, I converted to speed and put myself a mile and a half in trail, co-altitude.

"Challenger, I don't see you, say your position."

"Dead six, mile and a half."

The next thing I saw was one of the most amazing things I have ever witnessed. The Tomcat pilot, now knowing full well my position, was not about to let himself get shot out of the sky from a straight and level cruise position. One moment I was looking at the stern profile of his aircraft; in what seemed like the next millisecond, I saw the full silhouette of his plane from the top with his wings sweeping forward.

I began to pull to try to stay with him. Fat chance!

We ended up in a rolling scissors in close combat. I would go across the top while he scooted across the bottom. He truly had the advantage, but I was not going to give up without a fight.

As I would come across the top and pull my nose down, I would accelerate to well over 500 knots. And there he was! So close! All I had to do was pull my nose up and put him in my gunsight!

I could feel my wings full of lift. I felt as though the aircraft was an extension of my body. I only had to pull, just a little bit more, to get my nose pointed at the Tomcat. Then I could have my victory.

Unfortunately, my Skyhawk did not have it in her. Even though I had the nose pointed straight down into the Caribbean Sea with more than 500 knots on the airspeed indicator, each time I pulled on the stick, the wing moved from a flying condition into critical angle-of-attack. She would buck and shudder and threaten to depart controlled flight if I didn't straighten up and treat her right.

Eventually, the Tomcat pilot won.

When everyone hit bingo fuel and the Tomcats went back to the ship and the Skyhawks returned to Guantanamo, I reflected on what had just happened. Like many pilots, I had listened to the older pilots and flight instructors tell me how airplanes can stall in any attitude and at any airspeed.

Like most young pilots, I did not fully believe them.

Now I do.

Navigation

Getting around the world is a fascinating exercise. At first, a person's awareness of his or her environment is the extent of as far as they can see, usually not much further beyond their crib or bedroom. Then they discover the different rooms of their home. After that follows the discovery of the back yard.

Before long, they know their neighborhood and then their town. When they are in school, they learn about their state and that the state is part of a nation and the nation is only one of many on the globe.

In studying the globe, there are facts to memorize and once learned, those facts can help a person "get around." For instance, there are 360 degrees in a circle, and 60 minutes in every degree, which then gives you 60 seconds per minute. Since one degree equals 60 nautical miles, one minute will equal one nautical mile. Multiplying all of the degrees around the circumference of the globe (360 degrees x 60 minutes), you discover a trip around the world is 21,600 nautical miles. Multiplied by 1.15 to determine statute miles, the world around any greatest part, is 24,840 statute miles.

All pretty useless information, right?

Well, consider this.

The ancient Polynesians, after discovering the limits of their living quarters and then their islands, went from their island chain in the South Pacific, all the way across 5000 miles of open ocean to the middle of the Pacific to find Hawaii. Then they went home again. And back. They made this trip many times, thousands of years ago, before the development of navigational tools. Using their hands as rudimentary sextants and the stars, combined with knowledge passed down in song from one generation to the next, these ancient mariners canoed from their homes to the Hawaiian Islands many times.

Today, GPS gives us the ability to find the exact fishing hole in the middle of a lake or position ourselves repeatedly over the same reef in the ocean—within 10 feet of the last time we were on the position. It seems virtually impossible to get lost in these modern days of electronic navigation.

I remember one flight I flew in my A-4 out of Guantanamo Bay, Cuba. I was out patrolling when I came across a very interesting sight. There, on the surface of the Caribbean Sea almost equidistant from Cuba, Jamaica, and Haiti, was a dugout canoe with a couple of fishermen seeking their sustenance. I could barely see the land from my altitude of 2000 feet, so I knew they could not possibly see land from the surface of the sea.

How did they get there? I thought. And how many generations of their family carried on this tradition? More importantly, I wondered how they were able to find their way home.

Me? I had TACAN.

Impressions

I remember the first time I saw the Blue Angels. I was working on the line fueling Cessnas and Pipers at the St. Pete-Clearwater International Airport, so I was standing atop my fuel truck. I watched the team arrive and fly their practice session and then it was time for them to land.

I reasoned the pilots would take separation and land individually. I watched in amazement as the flight lead brought the six-plane formation around on final approach in the delta formation. The four planes of the diamond formation were in their normal positions, with solo pilots in the outer positions.

As they approached the runway, the lead aircraft was in the highest point of the delta formation and the three A-4s across the

The Diamond Formation

back, the lowest. All six airplanes moved as one; there were six right hands manipulating flight controls, six left hands moving power control levers, and 12 boots working rudder pedals. Seemingly, it appeared as if only one mind was flying all six jets.

Standing as high on the fuel truck as I could to see everything, I watched the delta approach for the actual touchdown. Each airplane held position as the formation came closer to the ground. All six tires of the three rear aircraft touched the runway at the same moment. Then their nosewheels touched.

Then the four mainmounts of the wingmen's jets screamed onto the runway. A half-heartbeat later, their nosewheels slammed down. Next, Lead's airplane came to the ground and the six planes were no longer flying.

As they seemed as one in flight, so now were they on the ground. It was the most impressive display of airmanship I ever witnessed. I suddenly realized why aviators throughout the world referred to these guys as "the best of the best."

Today's Blue Angels are as skillful and as disciplined as the first team led by LCDR Roy "Butch" Voris. Voris opened the very first show of The Blues at NAS Jacksonville in June 1946 flying F-6F Hellcats. Since then, only the airplanes seem to change — from the less sophisticated to more advanced. If you have the chance to see

High Speed Solo Pass

the Blue Angels fly this year, don't miss it. Each year, their final performance is their homecoming show at NAS Sherman Field in Pensacola, FL.

Seeing what I witnessed that day back in 1976 compelled me to compete for a seat in the fleet. That was the true job of The Blues — to spread the excitement and enthusiasm for naval aviation among the nation's youth. To that end, they are extremely effective and successful.

The Navy charged today's team of Blues with the same job as CDR Voris' 1946 team. Surely they convinced more than a few young men and women to compete for a seat as naval aviators.

Ed's Hotrod

Occasionally a pilot will ask which airplane I liked flying the best in the Navy. The answer I always give is, "Depends. If I was going out to deliver weapons, no question — it is the A-7. If I was going out to fly for fun, it is the A-4."

Both airplanes were great fun to fly. The A-7 was a workhorse compared to the A-4 in terms of the load it could carry, but if you were going to go fly and just rip around the sky, nothing was better than Ed Heinemann's little hotrod.

The A-4 taught generations of naval aviators a lot about flying. Many of us completed our "Strike" training in the TA-4J Skyhawk to attain our Wings of Gold.

The A-4 first flew on June 22, 1954 and enjoyed a production run until 1979. During that time, Douglas Aircraft delivered almost 3000 airplanes to various military forces, including 555 two-seat trainers.

Douglas supplied variants of the aircraft to fit the needs of the Marines for electronic warfare and their specific attack mission. During Vietnam, the A-4 was one of the mainstays of naval aviation, flying from the decks of carriers in the Gulf of Tonkin against targets in North Vietnam.

The airplane really was a kick in the pants to fly. She had a maximum speed of 585 knots (673 mph) powered by a Pratt & Whitney J-52. A pair of drop tanks could take the airplane almost 2000 miles. The airframe was good for -3g up to +8g. One of the most spectacular things the airplane could do well was roll. At the best working speed, she could roll 720 degrees per second.

The memories I enjoy most of the airplane involve lots of speed, lots of g, formation flying, shooting guns and missiles, and dropping bombs. The airplane did all of those things with aplomb. I particularly enjoyed dropping things.

For instance, the airplane did commendably as a manual bomber dropping Mk 82 general purpose bombs. To go out with a couple of TERs (triple ejector racks) with three Mk 82s each and drop a couple of bulls eyes on the bombing range was very satisfying. It is similar to going to a pistol and rifle range and practicing your marksmanship—the difference between shooting and bombing is that in the case of bombing, you sort of ride the bullet for a while on the way to the target.

Something else I really enjoyed with the airplane was air combat maneuvering (ACM), otherwise known as dogfighting. ACM is like a huge three dimensional game of chess. In chess, there is a lot of thinking taking place in your cranium when you go up against an opponent. In ACM there's a lot more mental activity combined with science, physics, physical brawn, and patience—a lot of patience.

Don't be misled by the idea of patience in a dogfight. Most dogfights only last about 30 seconds, to maybe a minute, or a minute and a half perhaps. During that time, however, the concept of time stands almost completely still. And this is where the idea of patience comes into play. For a fighter pilot to take advantage of his opponent and win, he has to carefully fly the airplane on the edge of the performance envelope. Combat pilots must be patient with small gains on their opponent until saddling into the kill position.

All of this was a challenge and extremely fun. Yeah, sometimes it was a little dangerous, sometimes it was a little scary, and I am sure mothers of naval aviators all over the world don't understand or like it one bit.

But for those of us flying airplanes like Ed's hotrod, nothing was more rewarding.

Blue Diamond A-4Cs

Luvin' Speed

Speed is a relative concept. Airplanes go fast—and slow. Many consider sailboats slow, but yachtsmen can sail them fast. Cars simply take forever to get anywhere, unless the driver is a teenager. Then it is probably just plain frightening.

When I was a kid, I liked to drive fast. This was in the days before I studied physics and had little idea of how speed can be so dangerous (you know, it's that mass and velocity relationship—particularly when it comes to stopping).

After a stint as a news reporter-photographer where I had to go on assignment to auto accidents and saw the results of the damage speed could cause firsthand, I started to get smart and slow down. I still liked speed, though, even if it might be a little dangerous.

While learning how dangerous speed is, I also learned about risk management. Then I discovered all you had to do when going really fast was manage the risk. After learning this and thinking about it a bit more, I was back to enjoying speed. Legally in the air, rather than speeding along the highways.

Luckily for me, I flew bigger and faster airplanes as my thirst for speed increased.

I thought of becoming an airline pilot. Airliners could go fairly fast. Indeed, with a good jetstream on your tail, you could clock across the country at better than 750 knots. There was only one problem. From up at Flight Levels, it does not seem as though you are going fast, even though you really are.

Up there, you sit looking over all the terrain below, sometimes for hundreds of miles. If not for the DME, pilots might not realize they are flying so fast. I spent enough time as a passenger to know I wanted more action than Flight Level speed. This led me to the military; it was in the military where I found the best and fastest airplanes. While serving in the Navy, I found the best job for enjoying my penchant for going fast: low-level attack pilot. What a blast!

From an airliner, looking down at the Sierra Nevada is tantamount to looking down from the top of your roof at children's "mountains" in their sandbox in the backyard. From altitude, you can see the Sierra Nevada mountains meeting up with the Cascades, stretching all the way from Mexico to Canada, far below. From the cockpit of an attack jet, the mountains are an entirely different sight.

On the ingress to the target, an attack pilot uses the mountains to hide. The pilot stays low behind hills and mountains. When crossing over a ridge line, attack pilots roll their aircraft inverted, pulling 3g to 5g to just clear the ridge by no more than a couple of hundred feet. The reason is to keep positive g on the airplane; additionally, if you tried to push over the top of the ridge, you would not be able to see where you were going with the nose in the way — it may cause you to run into a rock on the other side. It truly is the best fun a human can experience. At 540 knots. Roughly nine nautical miles per minute. Or 622 mph.

Yeah, I still like speed, but not on the roads. There are too many crazy drivers out there and one of them just might kill you.

Naw, speed on the highway is just way too dangerous.

The Navy Corsairs

Whenever someone mentions the name "Corsair," most aviation enthusiasts immediately think of the inverted gull-winged F-4U Corsair from World War II. A few will think of the A-7 Corsair which gained fame as a light attack bomber in Vietnam. Even fewer know of the existence of the O2U or SU-4 Corsair, the very first of the Corsairs.

The O2U, produced by the Vought Corporation in the mid to late 1920s, served the Navy, Marines, and Coast Guard as an observation platform. Construction of the airplane consisted of conventional steel tubing, wood, and fabric. A Pratt & Whitney R-1340 Wasp engine producing 400 horsepower powered the

The First Corsair

airplane. Many of the Corsairs served as seaplanes and a few were actually amphibious.

Later in the 1930s, Vought further developed the airplane to include an upgrade to the 600 horsepower Pratt & Whitney R-1690 Hornet engine. The Navy also re-designated the airplanes as the SU-4, putting them into the role of scouts. Performance of the airplane was typical of the biplane era. The airplane had a maximum speed 167 mph and a range of only 680 miles at a considerably slower cruise speed. The airplane served the Navy through the 1930s. When Japan forced the United States into war in 1941, the fleet still maintained 141 of the biplane SU-4 Corsairs.

The most famous of the Corsairs, the F-4U, began its reign in February 1938 after the Navy requested proposals for new fighters. Naval officials wanted an airplane with the fastest possible forward speed and a stall speed less than 70 miles per hour. They also wanted it to carry four guns and be capable of dropping bombs. In 1938 and 1939, Vought designed and produced a mockup of the XF4U-1 Corsair.

The new fighter had a Pratt & Whitney XR-2800 prototype engine. The engine produced over 1800 horsepower and later became the Double Wasp engine of 2000 horsepower. The first flight of this Corsair took place on May 29, 1940. The pilot, Lyman Bullard, terminated the flight early because of aerodynamic flutter with the elevator trim.

The Navy encountered other problems with the airplane during carrier suitability trials. Even after they resolved the problems, many still considered the airplane "a handful" for the less experienced pilots. As always, naval aviators proved adaptable and the airplane went on to become one of the most successful fighters of World War II and Korea.

The Bent Wing Corsair

The last airplane to carry the moniker "Corsair" for the U.S. Navy was the A-7 series. Vought designed the A-7 Corsair II light attack aircraft as a replacement for the A-4 Skyhawk. Initial work on the design commenced in 1962. Vought based the design of the aircraft on the F-8 Crusader. Compared to the Crusader, the Corsair was shorter, less powerful, slower, and stubby in appearance. Many also considered the airplane "uglier."

Beginning in 1967 and through 1971, 27 Skyhawk squadrons converted from the A-4 to the new A-7s. In that first year, VA-147 based aboard the *USS Ranger*, took the airplane into combat for the first time in Vietnam.

The Corsair II served the United States Navy well from Vietnam, to Granada, Libya, Panama, and Iraq. The Navy retired the last of the Corsairs in 1991 when the last A-7Es returned home from Desert Storm.

The A-7E Corsair II

Tips and Techniques

Flying Tired

For some jobs, working tired is a real inconvenience. For others, however, trying to do your job tired could become lethal. These are jobs such as driving trucks, running an operating room, fighting fires, walking a police beat, commercial fishing, and my personal favorite—flying airplanes.

Each time I think of airplanes flown by tired aircrew, the one accident that comes to mind and one I discuss with my students at length happened in Guantanamo Bay, Cuba. Kalitta International Flight 808 was a cargo flight scheduled from Norfolk, VA to Naval Air Station Guantanamo Bay on August 18, 1993.

Because of the length of the flight, the "surprise" assignment to the crew, and the inadequacy of the crew duty and rest requirements, the crew was flying the airplane well beyond the time they should have been in the chocks. Consequently, the pilot-in-command's judgment and flying abilities were affected. The skills of the other two crewmembers were also similarly impacted.

Because of the scheduled departure and arrival times, the three crewmembers were awake for an extraordinary amount of time before the accident. The flight engineer was up 21 hours, the second officer 19 hours, and the captain was awake for 23.5 hours. They were not at their prime on arrival at NAS Gitmo at approximately 5 p.m.; due to their degraded performance, the crew lost the airplane on the approach to Runway 10 at Leeward Point.

The Douglas DC-8 freighter crashed at four minutes prior to 1700 local time. The impact destroyed the aircraft and all three crew were seriously injured. According to the findings of the National Transportation Safety Board (NTSB), the captain reported he "felt very lethargic or indifferent." He went on to further state he could not remember making power changes or performing the base to final turn. Obviously, he had lost his ability to focus on the tasks at hand.

Many drivers have experienced this phenomena as well; nodding off while driving, not truly being aware of their surroundings. It is not a good condition while driving; it is certainly not the manner in which a professional flight crew should be operating a 100-ton or heavier airliner.

If you are a pilot, think about your crew rest requirements and do not break them. If you are motoring down the road, think about the consequences of driving tired. Don't do it!

It is not worth the risk.

Me? Right now, the worst thing I may suffer is passing out in the middle of this sentence and going face down in the keyboard of the computer. That could be bad, but not fatal.

Eventually, I would wake up and go to bed.

Technology

The technology we have today is amazing. With each passing day, I marvel at the new inventions, perfected by someone only yesterday, or this morning, just to make this evening more wonderful.

Often I tell my students I am too old, and I am too young. I would have enjoyed being a part of The Greatest Generation; I think they had the most fun of all, even though they got the shortest end of the stick when it came to the world situation. I would also like to be young enough, or sufficiently cognitive in my later years, to see the wonderful new technologies of the next 50 years. I have always felt I was born too late, or too early. That's my story and I'm sticking with it.

In both my fields, writing and flying, the technological advancements over the last 40 years has been phenomenal. In 1975, *yes, 1975*, one of the professors at the School of Journalism at the University of Florida, stood before us and said, "Newspapers are dead." Not the thing to say to a bunch of aspiring news reporters.

He went on to say the news of the future was going to come into every household through a device, "Not quite a television set, but something similar," he theorized. Those of us in the classroom did not have kind things to say about this professor; many of us thought he was an idiot and wondered where he could have garnered such information. There was no way the newspapers of America could possibly die — they were the backbone of our journalistic system. Everyone knew television reporting only gave the audience the minor details of an event and the real meat of a story could only be found in a newspaper article.

In aviation, when I started training for my instrument rating, I flew airplanes woefully inadequate for instrument flight by today's standards. And I did this "in the soup." In bad weather. In the clouds! From a place I could not see where I was going more than half the time I was flying.

In those early days, our primary means of navigation included the VHF omnidirectional system, or VOR. At that time, most airplanes used in training had only one VOR receiver. This meant navigating along your course, momentarily switching frequency to another station, identifying that station, and determining the radial you were crossing. Then you would go back to the original frequency and continue along your route.

By the 1980s, many airplanes were equipped with high quality and redundant radios. And then we began to see other systems coming on line. Area navigation (RNAV) was brilliant! Distance measuring equipment (DME) was wonderful. Radios became more reliable and pilots did not have to rely on that 7700 for one minute, 7600 for the next 14, and fly the last of the "assigned, expected, or filed."

Today we have GPS—and almost every little kid and his or her grandmother knows it is Global Positioning System. Not only is this technology amazing in the airplane, I can't believe I can take a portable unit to my car and ask it where the nearest gas station might be, or the nearest movie theater—and it knows! For every location in all the United States!

How is this possible? And how did live without these things before?

The Importance of Reading

Something slowly disappearing from the repertoire of many individual skills is the art of reading. Today, too many people are attached to their electronic devices. The idea of reading a book has fallen from popularity. It takes too much time, there are too many pages, it is too hard. How many other excuses are there...let me count the ways.

When it comes to reading, it is all about interpretation. Personal interpretation. What one may read in a particular passage will mean something very different to another reader. Additionally, when reading an instructional text, the reader has to reflect on the written knowledge, embedding it in memory for use later. How well this "embedding" is done will determine how well and however long the student can use the information.

One aspect, one very pleasurable aspect of reading, is that you can lose yourself in a story. Many young people today lack this wonderful experience and skill; they have never read a novel or an autobiography or biography they truly enjoyed. Consequently, they have not yet realized this level of pleasure in reading.

Back in grade school, one of the first serious books I read was Ted W. Lawson's *Thirty Seconds Over Tokyo*. Lawson was one of the 80 volunteers who flew with Jimmy Doolittle on April 18, 1942 in the first raid against the Japanese homeland following the attack on Pearl Harbor. The book, co-authored by newspaperman Robert Considine, was well-written. The work flowed eloquently, logically, and simply from the first page to the last.

I was lying in my bed reading the book and had reached the point where Lawson and his crew were running out of both gas and daylight at the same time. It was a bad situation and they decided to land their B-25 on a beach on the China coast. They dragged the beach once, turned downwind, dirtied up the plane and planned the approach.

Then the worst thing that could possibly happen did. Both engines quit on short final and they crashed into the ocean a quarter mile from the beach. Everyone was injured — the tail gunner, David Thatcher the least, and Lawson, the worst.

In the crash, Lawson's left leg was gashed open almost the entire length of his thigh down to the femur. I was so engrossed in the story that when my mother asked me to take out the garbage, I almost yelled back, "Mom, I can't! My leg hurts too much."

This is what I mean by "getting into the story."

The really nice thing about reading "in depth" to this degree is that the experience of the writer telling the account will stick with the reader a long time. This is what is known as "vicarious learning" and it is important in learning how to fly.

Student pilots must read a lot of aviation textbooks — that's a given. Some of that reading, no, a lot of that reading, can be dull and boring. This is why it is so important to read other books, both fiction and nonfiction, about flying.

If a pilot can learn about flying from other pilots who have written of their experiences, they can learn and reinforce aviation concepts through a good story. Legitimately. The first time I learned the concepts of weight and balance, density altitude, and aircraft loading was through reading Ernest K. Gann's *Fate is the Hunter*.

If you are in need of aviation reading, may I suggest our website, BluewaterPress LLC (*www.bluewaterpress.com*)? There, you will find a list of some of my favorite aviation texts, along with a fairly extensive aviation fiction and nonfiction titles.

Why You Should Fly That Old Taildragger

My friend, Shelly, is fond of saying, " 'Bout the time you start feeling comfortable and think you have everything under control, you suddenly see a bright flash going by the right side of your cockpit. A split second later, you realize what you actually saw was the tail of your airplane flashing past."

I chuckle every time I hear him tell that yarn; deep in my heart, I know he speaks the truth. I have been that hapless pilot wondering what that thing outside the cockpit window might be, only to realize it was my tail. As with gear up landings, there is the school of thought that there are those who have and those who will—groundloop a tail-dragging airplane. If you are lucky, as I have been, no damage will result other than to your pride. If you are unlucky, well, the damage can be very costly in terms of repairs.

Many modern-day pilots who learned to fly in Cessnas and Pipers with nosewheels have a hard time understanding why taildragger pilots sometimes seem distant and aloof, as if they are privy to a private joke. They do not understand why some tailwheel pilots might ignore the opportunity to fly a twin with a glass cockpit, but will jump at the chance to fly an antique biplane or old Cub with the door open.

Tailwheel airplanes are demanding from engine start to shut down. Because of the inherent instability of the landing gear design, pilots quickly learn to control the forces acting on the aircraft's center of gravity and how to keep the longitudinal axis perfectly aligned with the runway without drifting. The truth is this: in his or her heart, tailwheel pilots know they can fly just about any airplane ever built. On the other hand, nosewheel pilots cannot.

This is the point where many nosewheel pilots become indignant with tailwheel pilots; there is, however, a corollary truth to the idea of learning to fly in taildraggers and learning to drive with a standard transmission. Take the driver who learned how to drive in a 1969 Volkswagen Bug. The Bug has a standard transmission with four on the floor and a third pedal called a clutch.

It takes a bit of practice to become smooth at driving old Bugs, but once mastered, the Bug driver can drive anything with a standard transmission... or with an automatic transmission for that matter. However, the driver who learned how to drive on a late model Chevy with an automatic transmission is pretty well limited only to vehicles with... well, automatic transmissions.

The same holds true of a pilot who learns to fly in taildraggers. Once mastered, the pilot who can deftly handle a taildragger can certainly fly anything with wings, no matter the landing gear arrangement.

Now, if you are one of those pilots who learned in a Cherokee or a 172 and you want to increase your skill level, find someone who teaches in a Champ or Cub. Train for your tailwheel endorsement and afterward, fly that old taildragger for about 50 hours.

Fifty or so hours in an old airplane without radios will make you a far better pilot than you can imagine. You will also probably have so much fun you will fly that airplane a lot longer than a mere 50 hours.

Afterward, you too, will be one of those pilots passing up multis with glass for old antiques. I would bet on it.

Engine Failures

I told the story of my first engine failure in Joe's Luck (see page 7). Looking back from the vantage point of 30 years, it's pretty funny.

At the time, however, it lacked any humor; it was not until I slept on it that I began to see the wit of the situation.

Of course, engine failures are not a laughing matter. However, they don't have to be as serious as some pilots, the public, and most certainly, the news media, tend to view them. Handled correctly, an engine failure in a light single-engine airplane may be nothing more than a simple inconvenience. Keep in mind, *if handled correctly*.

So how do you handle an engine failure in an airplane correctly?

First, keep your head. Secondly, be well trained and follow through on your training. And finally, stay cool, calm, and collected.

Now, I will tell you the secret for accomplishing these three tasks. If you are well rested, properly hydrated, and eating well, you should have no problem with any emergency that comes your way. When you have had enough sleep and can think clearly, you are rested. Rest is one of the most important factors in being able to reason and use your intellect during a crisis. When it comes to hydration, keep in mind this means water. You know, that H_2O stuff, the clear liquid which makes up most of our bodies. Without it, your brain will short circuit and malfunction. This is something you do not need in the middle of an emergency. As much as we may wish, carbonated and caffeinated beverages do not qualify as proper liquids for purposes of hydration. Finally, you have to eat well if you are to keep your body primed for any emergency. This means taking in the proper number of calories spread out over the entire day. Additionally, the calories have to come from foods legitimately good for you. You know, those food groups your mom and dad tried making you eat when you were younger. Fast foods and milkshakes will not cut it this business.

Now, here are the brass tacks in dealing with engine failures.

When the engine fails at altitude, the most important thing you need to know is the wind direction. Always land the airplane into the wind. In order, these are the procedures you have to accomplish immediately. First, pitch the nose down and use your trim to set the correct glide speed. Next, pick a place to land while keeping the wind direction in mind in order to plan your approach and landing as close as possible into the wind. Finally, check proper positioning of the fuel valve; turn on the fuel boost pump. If the engine quit when the carburetor heat was off, pull it on and if it was on, push the control in. Try switching to each magneto independently; one mag may have failed and the other is perfectly fine. This is a generic list of procedures; remember to follow all of the recommended procedures in the pilots operating handbook (POH).

After completing these three items, and only if you have time, now you can talk on the radio. Make certain you do all those other things first. Remember, the rule is to aviate, navigate, and then communicate.

Remember that talking on the radio is way down on the list of priorities.

You Are Cleared to Blah, Blah, Blah

There is something I don't understand about the new pilots who are learning to fly these days. Many are all for flying, but they must have the radio to do it. And GPS. They can't go anywhere without their "technologies."

I don't know how many times I have talked with a new pilot about flying and asked, "Why do you fly?"

"Oh, I just love the freedom," they respond.

"You do?" I ask. "Then why do you give up your freedom to an air traffic controller?"

"What do you mean? You have to talk on the radios to be safe."

Deep down inside, I want to laugh…and cry. I know this new pilot is only reflecting and echoing the sentiments of his training, and I feel sorry for him. While he enjoys the "freedom" of flying, he has no clue as to what real freedom is all about.

I am willing to bet he has never shown up alone at the airport early in the morning just before the sun broke the horizon, while the dew was still thick and wet on the ground. He has missed the joy of pre-flighting, starting, and taxiing out to takeoff into a glorious sunrise. He may never have experienced flying through the smoothest air God ever created. I am sure he has never enjoyed the solitude of truly flying alone, of flying however high or low he desired, or flying whichever direction he chose — on a lark — just to be ... flying.

There is a certain delight in flying. The whole point in flying is to separate yourself from the earth, to traverse freely at your slightest whim. Today, many new student pilots believe you have to talk to ATC in order to fly "correctly" or "safely." Flight instructors are teaching these students you can only be safe when talking with someone on the ground. In essence, pilots today are giving up their freedom to ATC, which then tells them how fast, which direction, and how high they might fly. Doesn't sound too free, does it?

Often a new pilot will retort ATC keeps them clear of other traffic. Again, I go through the laughing-crying emotion. I want to scream, "Get your head up and out of the instrument panel and use your eyeballs to keep yourself clear of other airplanes! That's *your* job, not ATC's!" Then I think back on my own career and too many memorable near misses come to mind. Out of seven, ATC was involved in six of those events. In other words, ATC was the direct link which almost caused the collisions. Only one near miss occurred without the help of an air traffic controller.

Unfortunately, many of the nation's flight instructors today are teaching reliance on technology and the ATC system instead of self-reliance. CFIs need to focus on the basics and teach their students how to fly and how to think for themselves. Pilots need to listen to the voices in their heads and learn how to survive in the aeronautical environment, without depending on voices on the other side of a radio frequency.

If the instructors do that, and their students become very well qualified pilots, then maybe the voices on the other side of the radio can help make a safe pilot even safer.

"Go Ahead, Punk, Make My Day!"

I am dreaming. I know I am asleep and this is only a dream. In the dream, I see Dirty Harry threatening me with his famous line, "Go ahead, punk, make my day!" Only Dirty Harry is not a cop, and I am not a bad guy. And the powerful handgun he is holding, the .357, is not really a weapon. The dream I am having does not deal with criminals, cops, and gunfights; Dirty Harry is a metaphor for something bad that is about to happen and the bullet from the .357 is the allegory consequence to hitting the ground — really hard.

Every pilot worth their salt should have thought about this situation. Engine failure on takeoff. It is the only time I truly fear engine failures. An engine failure at altitude really is of no consequence. If the engine fails enroute, you merely pitch and trim to the proper glide speed, find a place to land, try to restart, and then land if you don't get it running again. Engine failure on takeoff? Well, let's just say that's a little different.

I will submit to you that young and inexperienced pilots have on occasion, turned the airplane back to the runway with success. I will also say they were probably very lucky.

Ask any group of pilots what to do with an engine failure at 600 feet above the ground on takeoff and you will find some who will say, "Turn back."

Then ask the question, "What bank angle would you use?" Some will respond with "a shallow turn" because you don't want to bank too much close to the ground. Others will respond with "turn steeply" to get the turn over with in as little time as possible in order to preserve altitude.

Neither response is correct. If you are going to turn back to the field, you must use exactly a 45-degree angle-of-bank (AOB) turn; this accomplishes both objectives of turning quickly while preserving precious altitude.

Here is something else to think about, also. Each year, I stand in front of many young pilots and tell them with my 43 years of experience and thousands of hours of flight time, if I were to have an engine failure at 600 feet on takeoff, there is no way I would attempt returning to the airport. Following an engine failure on takeoff, I would immediately lower my nose, look no more than about 30 degrees left or right of my flight path, then I would pick the path of least resistance and land.

A few points to keep in mind regarding the engine failure and the turn back to the field: first, you are going to be startled and the process of accepting the fact of the engine failure may take too many precious seconds. Secondly, trying to turn the airplane back to the airport will take Chuck Yeager-like flying skills, something that will be hard to come by during the middle of an emergency. Third, keep in mind stall speed increases 14 percent at 40 degrees AOB, 41 percent at 60 degrees, and a whopping 140 percent at 80 degrees.

Now, combine an uncoordinated turn with the high stalling speed and you have the classic recipe for a fatal stall-spin accident. If the airplane stalls in the middle of the turn back to the runway with the ball to the outside of the turn, the airplane will enter a spin, a spin from which there is not enough altitude to recover. Impact with the ground will be harsh and out of control compared to a landing straight ahead.

By landing straight ahead, the airplane is flying into the wind and impact velocity is controlled and minimal. Stalled and spinning out of low altitude turn, however, puts the airplane in a situation where impact velocity with the ground is high and the aircraft is out of control. All pilots need to keep in mind that the more the impact is controlled, survival becomes a higher probability.

Me, if I have a complete engine failure on takeoff, I'm taking it straight ahead. I'm good, but I know I am not Chuck Yeager or Bob Hoover good — and never will be.

Cutting Teeth

I am nervous, the weather is not good. I have been contracted to fly a client in her airplane, a Cessna 182, to the Cook County Airport at Adel, GA. The weather in Tampa is awful, below mins. And I am a new commercial pilot with an untested instrument rating. How did I get myself into this mess?

I talk with the weather-liars, uh, I mean, briefers. They explain all the dynamics of what is creating the weather in the southeast and they tell me Valdosta is 200 OVC ½ mile. Then the briefer says, "But by the time you get there, they are calling for 700 to 800 broken to scattered with two miles or better."

Uhmmm. As long as the mighty Continental O-230 keeps purring while we fly over the bad weather, we should not have a problem. I feel comfortable with his forecast, except for the part about flying over the undercast. I know the weather below is solid cloud and fog all the way to the ground. If the engine fails, it is not going to be good. But I have been flying the airplane for a while in good weather, and the Continental has been smooth and steady the whole time. Uhmmm.

I pick up my IFR clearance and depart. The client is in the backseat with her work spread around her. I am up front doing my pilot thing. The skies are clear, except for the undercast, which is fairly thick. We're cruising at 6000 and it looks as if the tops are about 2000. The further north we go, the more I listen to Flight Watch. Then I start listening to VLD ATIS.

The more I listen, the more ATIS validates my perception that anyone associated with weather prognostics is an outright liar. They said, "700 to 800 feet broken to scattered with two miles viz." The reality is still 200 overcast with half a mile — at best. It is time for an ILS and while I have done plenty as an IFR student in good weather under the hood, I have never done one in real life. With real mins. With real visibility down at one half a mile... I give my passenger the bad news that we are going to have to land in Valdosta and she will have to rent a car to get to Adel.

Over the years since becoming a flight instructor, I have counseled my new instrument charges not to do what I am about to do. I always tell my new instrument pilots, "Go out and fly in lower weather conditions and get some experience before going to minimum conditions." I give them that advice from personal experience.

Now, I find myself at the outer marker about to enter the clag. Localizer's good, glideslope's alive. I am on the descent now. Passing 1000 feet, something odd happens. I go a little high on the glideslope and I can't get it back down. Try as I might, I cannot get the airplane back on the glideslope. I am about half-deflection high and I just cannot bring myself to increase the rate of descent to get back on the glideslope. I know the ground is somewhere down there.

I am now through 500 feet and looking for the runway and of course, there is nothing to see beyond the front of the airplane other than fog. I notice I am starting to go ever higher on the GS. This is not good. Now, I am 300 AGL according to the charts and the instruments. If the weather is right at 200 and I keep going higher, I might miss the airport.

Suddenly, I have the perception it is getting lighter around me. Then there it is, the end of the runway, appearing out of the mist like some ancient sailing ship coming into port through a sea fog.

Holy crap! The system really does work, I thought. *There's the runway!*

My passenger, who has not said a word the entire flight, now leans forward and says, "Can't you just follow Interstate 75 up to Adel?" The answer was, of course, no.

There was no doubt in my mind, this was the day I cut my teeth as a real instrument pilot.

Night Flight

"You want to fly at night? Well, you just go over to Tampa International or somewhere else to fly at night. I don't let my airplanes fly at night." Charlie looks at me like I have lost my mind. "But here's something I am going to tell you. That engine quits at night and you're going to wish you had a parachute."

I can understand what he means, about the parachute. It would be nice to have, if the engine failed at night. I remember reading about Lindbergh's account of running out of gas one night while flying the mail. He had a parachute and he used it. He jumped out of his plane and as he drifted down, the plane kept circling around threatening to hit him in the descent. It is a great story he tells in his book, *The Spirit of St. Louis.*

While his account was harrowing, Lindbergh also wrote well of flying at night. He was a descriptive writer and after reading about his night flights, a pilot who had not flown at night would be primed to explore. Which is what I want to do. I want to experience everything I can in aviation, including flying in the dark.

Charlie placated me for a while with his comment about wanting a parachute if the engine failed. It made sense; if you were flying around in the dark and the engine quit, it might be hard picking a good place to land. For the longest time, I thought about that scenario. Just what would you do in case the engine quite in the dark?

Later in my career, I would fly at night. It started a lot like Lindbergh's job of flying the night mail, only I was flying checks for the Federal Reserve as a contract pilot. After that, I flew in the Navy and of course, those guys fly regardless of the time of day.

Flying at night is serious business and if you are not instrument rated or equipped, I would think twice about it. Many of my professional pilot friends will not consider flying single-engine at night for the same reasons Charlie gave me over 40 years ago.

One day, I was heading home from a fly-in and my friend, Jim, a professional pilot with over 26,000 hours of flight experience watched me prepare for the flight. He knew where I was going and how long it would take to get there. He also knew what time I was departing and that I would spend the last hour flying in the dark.

"What are you doing?" he asked.

"Getting ready to head out."

"You know, it is going to be dark in less than an hour. And you're not going to be home before sunset."

"I know," I conceded.

"You know, the Bernoullis don't work in the dark, don't you? You're liable to fall right out of the sky." Jim wanted want me to stick around and share stories and drinks around the campfire with the other pilots, but I had to work in the morning. So I took off.

And it was a beautiful flight home, as in the case of most night flights flown on nights of clear weather. The moon was out and the stars helped show me the way home. The Continental C-145 up underneath the cowling droned steadily on, not missing a beat. But in the back of my mind, across all the years, distance flown, and flight time, I could still hear the old man's admonition.

"If that engine quits, you're gonna wish you had a parachute."

This Doesn't Feel Quite Right

I am sitting in the airplane with a pilot new to our FBO. He has come to get checked out to fly with us, so we are about to go up and I am going to watch him perform the perfunctory maneuvers and landings to see if he is safe enough to trust him with our airplanes. It will be just one of those typical flights.

After I watch him pre-flight, we are soon at the end of runway doing the pre-flight checks. He runs the engine up to 1700 rpm, checks the mags, and then pulls on the heat. Everything looks normal and then he turns to me and says, "That didn't feel right."

"What do you mean?" I ask.

"The carb heat control. Try it out."

I reach down and sure enough, it didn't feel right. There is a slight tug to the cable, a "chink" if you will. While the control did not "feel right," the engine operated normally and lost 100 rpm with carb heat applied. I look to the pilot and said, "Yeah, you're right. It doesn't feel right, but it is working. Your call."

"I guess it's OK," he said, continuing preparations for takeoff.

Moments later, we take off. Into a hot, humid morning, conditions of which puts us into the heart of the carburetor icing envelope.

At 200 feet agl, the engine sputters and the rpm drops to about 1800. It was a classic case of carb ice. The pilot looks of me as I reach for the carb heat control. I pull it out and the unthinkable happens. The cable comes off the carburetor heat box in the engine compartment and the next thing I know, I am holding the handle and the entire cable in the cockpit. The engine rpm remains at 1800, we are still at 200 feet, the airspeed has dropped to just under 55 knots, and now we are over houses.

Taking control of the aircraft, I make the shallowest, lowest, and slowest turns of my life. I pray the engine continues running. Luckily, we are the only aircraft in the pattern early this morning. Since the winds are calm, we can land opposite direction on the runway we just departed without incident — as long as the engine continues to run.

As we squeak over the trees at the end of the runway, a sense of relief rushes through my body. I take unusual delight in the sensation of the wheels touching down on the grass runway. We taxi over to the maintenance hangar and turn the aircraft in for repair.

As we preflight the next 150, we talk about the lessons learned from last flight. Even though this was a short flight, we both learned a great lesson by the time we had the airplane back on the ground. I would hear the phrase as a mantra later in my days flying in the Navy. "If it doesn't feel right, it's not right. Don't fly."

This flight from so long ago taught me valuable lessons. In addition to learning the key concept of not going if it doesn't feel right, I also learned there is no such thing as a typical flight.

Note: This was a partial power loss, not a full loss as discussed on page 101.

Running on Empty

Many have said there are three useless things in aviation. One is the altitude above you, the next is a runway behind you, and the third is the air in your fuel tanks. I am one to believe a pilot can never have too much fuel. How does a pilot come to feel strongly about this topic? Well, the short answer is you come too close running out of gas a couple of times in your career, and then you feel pretty strongly about keeping more gas.

As a civilian pilot, maintaining fuel levels is easier than in the military. When it comes to flying Cessnas and Pipers for fun, there is no excuse or any other reason to drive your fuel state down to unsafe levels. Sometimes, the tactical situation might drive a military pilot into cutting fuel margins too close. Another aspect about flying in the military is the horrendous fuel consumption of jet engines. In an hour and a half, I could burn up enough fuel to drive a typical sedan more than 45,000 miles.

According to the National Transportation Safety Board (NTSB), in the past 10 years about 150 pilots somehow mismanaged their fuel to the point of engine failure. Section 91.151 of Part 91 is specific about the fuel reserves required for visual flight rules (VFR) operations. A pilot must be able to fly beyond the destination, "assuming normal cruising speed-(1) During the day, to fly after that for at least 30 minutes; (2) At night, to fly after that for at least 45 minutes." Section 91.167 applies to instrument flights basically providing for fuel to the first intended destination, then to the alternate destination if required, and then 45 minutes beyond that.

For the new pilots out there, here is a heads up. Thirty minutes during the day and 45 minutes at night or for IFR operations is insane. Double those numbers! And that is at a minimum.

There are times when operational considerations may task you with carrying more fuel than required by 91.151 or 91.167. Common sense must prevail. Sometimes an enroute delay, the weather, or an accident at the destination airfield may consume every bit of your reserve and excess fuel beyond that.

Until you have been there, it is hard to imagine just how nervous the thought of running out of gas impacts your performance in the cockpit. In civilian life, I once got close to empty by accident. As a military pilot, I once landed with about 10 minutes remaining.

I guarantee two things about that military mission: first, it was not of my making and secondly, I nearly sucked up the seat cushion of the SJU-8 ejection seat on which I was sitting.

Coming Down

Want to be one of those pilots your friends and family will always want to fly with? Want repeat customers all the time? How do you do that? Well, you have to be smooth and one area in which smoothness really counts is getting the airplane down from altitude. If you are one of those pilots who yanks the power back and "screams" down from cruise altitude, no one will want to fly with you again, including your engine. By reducing power drastically and somewhat "diving" down, what you are doing is "shock-cooling" your cylinders. This will lead to cylinders or pistons cracking and very expensive engine repairs.

Proper planning for the descent is almost as important as planning fuel reserves. This area of flight planning is one pilots tend to ignore and one that provides great returns on investment when it comes to lower operating costs. It boils down to how you treat your airplane; treat it well, it will never let you down. However, if you abuse it, well, as they say . . . stand by.

If you are cruising at 7500 feet at a nominal cruise speed of 100 knots, you can use a 300 fpm descent profile to get down. Planning that descent takes a little finesse that goes beyond just checking out the charts in the book. There are more reasons than one why a 300 fpm is beneficial. First, an easy descent provides your passengers the greatest comfort regarding ear-popping pressure changes. Almost anyone can handle 300 fpm. Secondly, it helps minimize your engine expenses.

When it is time to descend, you need only adjust the elevator trim down slightly. Do not reduce the power. The airplane will accelerate slightly, but keep the power on the engine to allow for constant cylinder head temperatures. The big trick to this is planning the point at which to start the descent.

Assuming you want to be near pattern altitude about five miles from the airport to decelerate to pattern speed, your equation for let down planning will look something like this:

Start altitude:	7500 msl
Pattern altitude:	1000 msl
Altitude to lose:	6500 feet
Descent rate in fpm:	300 fpm
Time in descent:	21 min 40 seconds
Groundspeed in nm per minute:	1.67 nm/min
Distance required:	36.2 nm
Distance to airport:	5.0 nm
Descent point from destination:	41.2 nm

Planning problem for descent at 100 kts gs

Forty-one miles away for the descent point is quite a distance. Keep in mind that is for an old, stodgy Cessna. If you fly something sportier such as an RV-7 or Mooney, look at the numbers for those airplanes that cruise roughly 180 knots, or three miles per minute.

Start altitude:	7500 msl
Pattern altitude:	1000 msl
Altitude to lose:	6500 feet
Descent rate in fpm:	300 fpm
Time in descent:	21 min 40 seconds
Groundspeed in nm per minute:	3.00 nm/min
Distance required:	65.0 nm
Distance to airport:	5.0 nm
Descent point from destination:	70.0 nm

Planning problem for descent at 180 kts gs

You can run the equation for different altitudes and airspeeds and the results may be surprising. It takes quite a bit of planning and real estate to get an airplane down from altitude.

New instrument pilots are quick to point out that ATC expects pilots to descend "as rapidly as possible" to within 1,000 feet of the target altitude and then at 500 fpm. While this is true, there are ways "to play the game" to allow you to get what you want. The tool for this is known as "pilot's discretion."

At your predetermined descent point, simply request a descent at pilot's discretion. Once the controller grants the request, you can descend at 300 fpm to the limit altitude. You may get clearance all the way to your requested altitude, or not. If you are limited to a higher altitude than requested, simply give them a couple of minutes lead by requesting a further descent when you are 600 feet above the newly assigned altitude. Typically, controllers can work with pilots with these types of requests.

By maintaining power and keeping engine temperatures constant, you can avoid costly trips to the maintenance hangar. More importantly, your passengers will thoroughly enjoy the ride.

Teaching Speed — The Basics

I have written about the extremes — flying high or low, fast or slow. I like the extremes and feel as if the heart of the envelope is, well..., boring from the standpoint of flying. When it comes to flying in the middle of the envelope, usually it means that you are just going somewhere. This is why you have to substitute the fun of flying for the excitement of navigation. More on that later.

So, teaching speed. If you are a young flight instructor, how do you help your students "get it?" What are the important points they should know about aircraft velocity? How does it relate to flying, aircraft loads, and safety?

First, we have to use a little correlation. Everyone who knows how to drive knows how to make a car go fast — you just mash on the gas pedal. In the airplane, you do the same thing; the pilot simply opens the throttle all the way by pushing the power lever into the instrument panel. On the highway, the car will go as fast as possible. In Florida, or on the dry lakebeds out west, the car will reach a maximum speed. On the level surface, you can only convert so much energy into speed.

In the airplane, the same concept is applicable. When the pilot opens the throttle all the way, the airplane can only go so fast *in level flight*. However, here is where the airplane pilot has the advantage over the automobile driver. If the pilot has altitude, he or she can put the nose down and go faster. In other words, they can dive the airplane to gain more speed if needed.

A driver cannot do the same in Florida or out on the dry lake beds. There are no hills, much less mountains in either location. In the mountains, however, the driver can go downhill and travel faster than the car is capable on level ground.

The opposite of this is going uphill. This is not possible for the driver in Florida or on the lake beds; again, there are no hills or mountains. In the mountains, however, there is the condition of driving up climbing roads. The driver will soon discover the car is not able to travel uphill as fast as it can on level ground. The steeper the uphill slope, the more horsepower is required to climb, leaving less horsepower to convert to speed. It happens exactly the same in the airplane. Only it is a little "different" in the airplane than in the car.

For the motorist trying to make it up a steep hill, the car will eventually run out of speed and stop as the incline increases. It will sit there on the side of the mountain and the motorist will set the brake, maybe turn off the engine, and then look around to enjoy the scenery.

The corollary scene in the airplane is quite different.

When the airplane pilot gets the nose going up too steeply, the airplane, like the car, will stop traveling uphill. Unlike the car, the airplane does not have a nice mountain road on which to sit when it stops flying. Instead, it falls out of the sky. We airplane pilots call this a stall. (For those reading who are not airplane pilots, stalls in aviation refer to the wing ceasing to fly, rather than the engine ceasing to run.)

Is a stall a big deal? No, not really, as long as there is plenty of space between the airplane and the ground for the pilot to start the airplane flying again. To do this, the pilot simply lowers the nose and the airplane is flying again—immediately!

Now, as a young flight instructor, here is the truly important part of your job. You must first explain, and then show your students that stalls are not a big deal. Many student pilots and younger, inexperienced pilots fear stalls. I was one of those. I did not like stalls at all. I had this fear of losing control of the airplane.

In truth, you never really lose control of the airplane. Sitting in the cockpit with the stick or yoke held full aft, you regain aerodynamic control of the aircraft the moment you move the stick forward. You are again in total control of the aircraft—you can choose when to fly and when to stall. When to fly fast, when to fly slow.

If you have full understanding of the airplane's speed envelope, you can maintain control going as fast, or slow, as the airplane is capable.

The Front Side and the Backside!

One of the more complex concepts for students or inexperienced pilots to grasp involves flying on the "front side" or the "back side" of the power curve. On the front side, everything seems to work correctly while on the back side, things work in "reverse." In this chart, the lower curve is the power required curve. The upper curve is the maximum power available curve. Where the two curves meet to the right, that is the maximum level speed the aircraft can fly.

The lowest point on the power required curve is where you will find the best endurance speed. This is the speed and power setting which is the minimum power is required to maintain level flight. Everything to the right of this speed falls in what we call the region of normal command. Speeds to the left, or less than best endurance, fall into the region of reverse command.

On the front side of the power curve, when you pull the nose up, you increase lift more than drag. Consequently, the airplane appears to behave "normally." In other words, when you pull

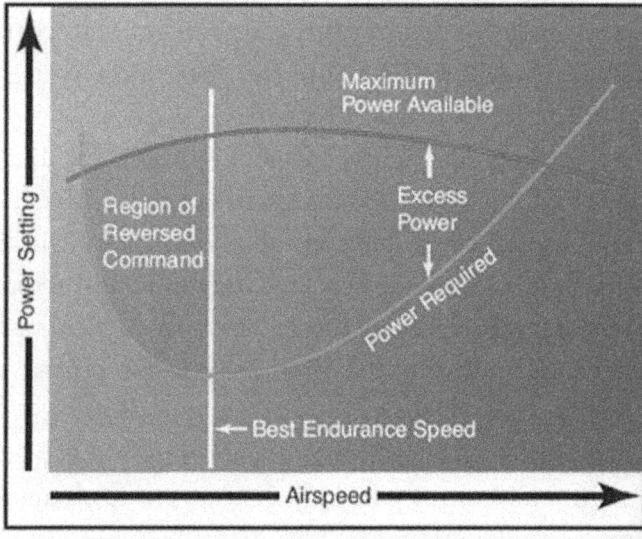

The region of reversed command

up the nose, the airplane goes up. Push down, and the airplane goes down.

On the backside of the power curve, or in the region of reverse command, things are different. If you have the aircraft stabilized at any speed less than best endurance, the airplane will behave in a manner which may seem odd. Essentially what happens is this: when you pull back on the stick increasing the angle-of-attack on the wing, you create more drag than lift. This causes the aircraft to descend, or "settle." To maintain level flight, you must increase power to compensate for the increased drag. If you do not increase the engine power, the aircraft will descend, even with the nose pointed higher. In this situation with fixed power in the area of reverse command, when you pull up the nose, the airplane will descend. If you lower the nose, the aircraft actually starts climbing because as airspeed increases, so does the lift.

The approach speed for most airplanes is near the best endurance speed. Most general aviation aircraft pilots, as well as airline pilots, will fly their landing approach at a speed on the normal side of the power curve. The aircraft responds more rapidly to pitch changes on the front side of the curve compared to the back side. Navy pilots flying tactical jet aircraft landing on ships must fly on the backside of power curve for specific operational considerations. Basically, they have to get slow enough to land on the ship and the placement of the tailhook depends on the high pitch attitude created by flying in the region of reverse command.

For most general aviation aircraft, the approach speed is near the best endurance speed. Adding a couple knots keeps the airplane on the front side of the power required curve. For new pilots, the thing to keep in mind is to be aware of where they are on the power curve during their approach to land.

And then push or pull appropriately, regarding pitch and power.

Stretching It

Following on the heels of writing about the power curves, I need to let you know how to "stretch it." Now, let me explain: I am not talking about stretching a glide or your gas supply. What I am referring to is getting the most miles per gallon from your available fuel.

Quite a few pilots have little idea of how to use their fuel most efficiently. It is quite an accomplishment to squeeze the last bit of mileage out of a drop of gas; I take great pride in getting 93,000 miles out of a set of 80,000 mile tires. It's the same with 100 octane low lead. The more hours I can fly on the fewer gallons of gas the better (especially at $5 to $7+ per gallon). Now let me explain, this has nothing to do with busting your reserves. Always, always carry enough fuel.

When it comes to flying, many inexperienced pilots are all about getting to their destinations as fast as possible. The movie Top Gun introduced the term, "I feel the need for speed." It seems to have become the mantra of young pilots today. I could never quite understand why student pilots, pilots who needed *to build* flight experience and log flight time, were flying around as fast as they could.

One day at the University of Florida, I witnessed a man who was about 70 years of age challenge a 21 year-old to a game of racquetball. The college student was not interested in playing the old man but the senior finally pestered the kid enough until the kid gave in. For all his youth, stamina, strength, and agility, I was very amused to watch the older gentleman use his skill and intellect to utterly destroy his youthful opponent by a score of 21 to 2. The poor student ran all around the court while the old man stood near the center of the court deftly popping the ball into the corners. He barely broke a sweat.

Flying a cross country should be the same way. Today's inexperienced pilots remind me of that college student using all muscle and brawn to go nowhere fast. The smart pilot, on the other hand, flies like the elderly racquetball player. He uses his street smarts to get the most out of his airplane.

For cross country planning, pilots should take advantage of altitude, power setting, and the winds to pinch out as much mileage as possible without using much of their fuel.

When it comes to altitude, 5500 to 8500 feet MSL is the most optimum performance altitude for cross country flying. The air is thinner and cooler up there, allowing the airplane to operate more efficiently, while providing a more comfortable ride for the pilot and passengers.

When it comes to the power setting, flying at higher altitudes naturally allows the engine to run at a lower power setting due to the lower air density. Consequently, the indicated airspeed is naturally closer to L/Dmax because of the thin air. With the airspeed nearer to L/Dmax, the airplane flies more efficiently.

Finally, we need to consider the winds. To get the most mileage out of your aircraft, look at the wind component as it relates to a headwind or a tailwind.

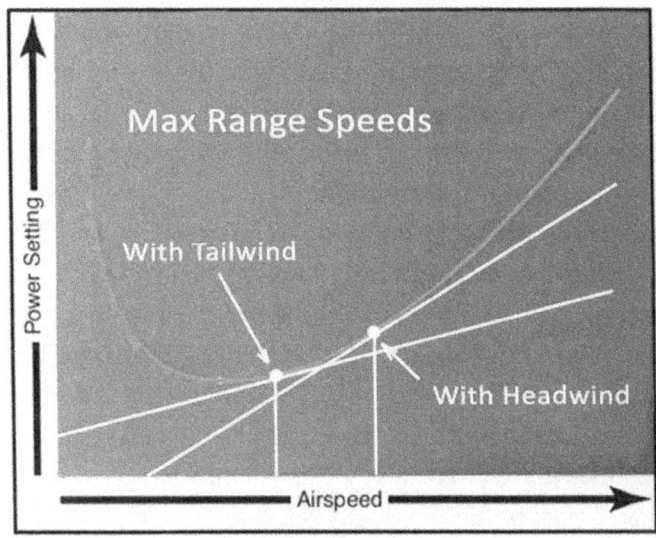

Wind Eff ects on Range

Going back to the basic power required chart, you can find the maximum endurance speed at the lowest point of the curve. The maximum range speed is determined by drawing a straight line from the origin until it intersects with the bottom of the power required curve. Now keep in mind, this velocity is only good in calm winds; if you have a tailwind, the line needs to originate at a point to the left of zero equal to the velocity of the wind. If you are fighting a headwind, you need to draw the line starting at the velocity of wind from a point to the right of zero.

What this means, is that with a tailwind, you will fly at a lower power setting to take advantage of the tailwind. With a headwind, you will find the best miles per gallon at a faster speed.

The Safety of "Little Airplanes"

Many question the safety of "little airplanes." General aviation aircraft have always been safe – extremely safe. In fact, flying privately owned airplanes is much safer than many may ever realize. Then why do so many crash? Are there a lot of crashes, or does it just seem so? Unfortunately, aircraft accidents always make the six o'clock news and the front page of the paper, no matter how insignificant or minor the accident.

The sad truth is this: About 40,000 people die on the nation's highways each year. Typically, less than 500 die in *all* aircraft accidents in the same period. Today, only one or two people may perish in an airplane accident. However, more than 109 Americans will perish on American highways! Yet, those 126 individuals will not have the story of their demise reach the front page of the newspaper? Why?

The reason is that as a society, we have come to accept death on the highway as a part of life. Highway fatalities are now commonplace. An airplane crash on the other hand, remains spectacular, a sometimes fiery event that thankfully, does not happen too often. Consequently, airplane crashes, always make the news because the accident sells papers and draws viewers to the evening news.

Regarding the safety of small airplanes, the pilot makes or breaks safety. General aviation safety is directly proportional to the operator's attitude. Just as with small boating, the careless skipper usually gets into trouble. If, however, the captain is knowledgeable in nautical regulations, skillful in the handling of the craft, and avoids unnecessary risks, the predictable conclusion of the sail is never in doubt. The same applies to general aviation.

The intelligence level of the participants in any field runs the typical bell curve — at each end of the curve, there are the two percent very gifted and the two percent who should never be allowed near an airplane. All the rest of us fall into the 96 percentile making up the middle of the curve.

As with any other sport, activity, or career, flying is only as dangerous as you make it.

The Art of Climbing

Getting to altitude involves more than getting into an airplane, starting the engine, and pointing the nose up. Pilots must consider many aspects factoring into the initial climb and the following ascent to cruise altitude. Some of these include the headwind or tailwind component, the climb corridor, clouds, and outside air temperature.

There is a great deal more to climbing an airplane than merely understanding the difference between V_x and V_y. Almost every private pilot and most student pilots understand the best rate of climb speed (V_y) gets you to altitude in the least amount of time. They also know the best angle of climb (V_x) attains the highest altitude gain over the shortest horizontal distance. Additionally, when it comes to actually getting to cruise altitude, the important question is which climb speed should be used.

For instance, every pilot knows in order to clear an obstacle at the end of a takeoff, the appropriate speed to use is best angle. They also know when it comes to climbing the airplane to altitude, the fastest way to get there is by using a V_y climb.

But what of the cruise climb? What is it and when should a pilot use it? What are the advantages to using cruise climb over the other climb speeds? Should the winds aloft be considered? How can a pilot best use different climb techniques for the most efficient use of the airplane?

When it comes to getting over obstacles, flight instructors teach student pilots short field take off techniques. This includes using every available foot of the runway, holding the brakes, running the engine to full power, releasing the brakes, accelerating to rotation speed with minimal angle-of-attack, and then rotating to a specific attitude — explicitly a pitch attitude resulting in the airspeed of V_x. Once clear of any obstacles, the pilot lowers the nose to allow the airplane to accelerate to either V_y or cruise climb. Nothing could be simpler, right?

Well...

Other considerations, such as making certain you don't get too slow is a very important. Sometimes the act of flying too slow occasionally appears in NTSB accident reports with the curt phrase, "Failed to maintain flying speed." This is why flight instructors and designated examiners pay very close attention to a student pilot's control of the aircraft during climb. They also want to make certain students and applicants are knowledgeable regarding the dangers of stalls and spins in this flight regime.

Beyond the initial climb concerns, the techniques used to get the airplane to cruise altitude involve safety and other operational issues. For instance, climbing the airplane at V_x involves a higher nose attitude, making it difficult for the pilot to see traffic out front. Fortunately, this climb does not last long. The V_y climb attitude is better, but can also hamper forward visibility. Flying a cruise climb at higher airspeeds affords better forward visibility but as with the two previous climb examples, also limits visibility to some degree.

The solution to seeing traffic over the nose is to gently S-turn throughout the climb. By turning the aircraft slightly, the pilot is able to clear in front of the nose prior to entering that airspace. This practice, as simple as it seems, can be life saving.

The wind is another consideration for climbing. If you are going to fly the majority of your flight with a headwind, don't be in such a hurry to get the airplane to altitude. The more time you spend with a headwind, the more fuel you'll burn. If on the other hand, you are going to be cruising with a tailwind, you will want to get up there as quickly as possible to take advantage of the tailwinds.

The Instrument Flying Season

We are moving into the "instrument time of the year." It is a precarious season, a season in which weather can be capricious at best and downright dangerous at worst. Caught in the middle with everything to lose or gain, is the newly instrument-rated pilot.

Many pilots think the most important thing to learn in working on an instrument rating is how to control an airplane on instruments. Actually, flying an airplane "on the gauges" is a skill a pilot can learn over time. The more important talent is knowledge of weather.

Before launching on a flight, the pilot needs to know what to expect regarding weather. This is easier for pilots who have lived in a particular region for any length of time as opposed to pilots operating somewhere they have never before flown. In other words, local pilots have a good feel for how the weather will behave, while transient pilots should pay more attention.

Since airplanes can go great distances in relatively short times, pilots should always be wary. Instead of being familiar with only their local weather, they need to get a feel for the dynamics of the weather happening within 500 miles or so of their position. They also need to analyze the type of weather they can fly through safely.

Every pilot knows the basics of weather, but the instrument pilot has to know the difference between inclement weather that is safe to fly in, compared to dangerous weather which might be deadly. For instance, working through an area influenced by a warm front with poor visibility, stable air, and stratus type clouds is a perfectly safe operation for a proficient instrument pilot. At the other extreme, trying to push through a cold front containing highly unstable air and associated thunderstorms could be lethal.

In addition to enroute weather, pilots must take a serious look at the forecasted weather for their destination at the time of their expected arrival. More importantly, they need to be able to shoot the approach for the actual weather on their arrival.

For weather consisting of semi-low ceilings requiring a non-precision approach, the ability to fly instruments down to 400 feet or so is not as critical as the skills required to fly a precision approach down to minimums of 200 feet with one-half mile visibility. The greatest difference between the two types of approaches is the time available to the pilot to set up for the landing after "breaking out," or acquiring visual cues to the landing area.

With the non-precision approach, minimum visibilities range between three-quarters of a mile to a mile and a half. On the precision approach, a pilot breaking out at 200 feet above the elevation of the runway with one-half mile visibility flying an approach speed of 90 knots has about 20 seconds for visual acquisition and transition to the landing.

While the flying side of the equation requires a high degree of knowledge and skill, the weather side of the equation is also critical. Knowing the weather not only involves a lot of knowledge about weather systems, but also requires judgment.

For pilots who have attained a skill level to allowing for comfortable flying while blind coupled with the knowledge of weather, there can be a no more versatile traveling vehicle than the private aircraft.

Low and Slow

Nothing is better or more fun than flying low and slow across the country. Particularly in an airplane with an engine that turns at a low rpm in cruise. It gives an all new meaning to the term "cross-county." Visit *www.vintageflying.com* to check out what flying low and slow is all about.

Typically, we fly because we have to get somewhere fast. In the haste of getting there, many have forgotten the joy of the journey; because we are travelling so rapidly, somehow the beauty of the countryside slowly slipping beneath our wings is a pleasure for which we have little time.

Most often, pilots file for high altitudes and they and their passengers have little inclination to look out the window. The airplane is so high above the ground, the details of the land are lost in the haze. While aircraft fly more efficiently "way up there," sitting inside an aluminum container is just no fun, compared to flying an airplane with an open window so close to the ground you can actually smell the odors of the earth.

In the course of teaching young pilots how to fly, we have moved away from the idea of flying for the sake of flying. Now, it is all about speed. The more the better. I have a love-hate relationship with the movie Top Gun, but that's a completely different story.

With more horsepower, young pilots have also realized finesse is no longer required. They can fly with less grace, skill, and elegance. If they get into a bad situation for a lack of their aeronautical knowledge or skill, they can power out of it with the airplane's oversized engine. Essentially, they have learned to use power as a crutch, rather than a tool.

In the "old days" when most airplanes had small engines and flew slower than 85 KIAS, pilots had to learn how to "fly the wing." Out of necessity, they were very careful to avoid pitching too high and they were always mindful of the angle-of-attack, particularly near the critical angle-of-attack.

The other consequence of powerful engines is higher fuel flows and increased operational costs. In pilot training, the higher airspeeds result in longer cross-country flights. The student still must meet the flight time requirement, but with larger and more powerful aircraft, the distance increases with the higher groundspeeds.

Basically, today's student pilots are missing some very important aviation lessons. The most critical of which is flying the wing.

They are also missing something else: the fun and joy of watching the ground slowly pass by underneath.

Headwinds

My wife and I spent a wonderful evening with friends one Saturday evening and then it was time to drive home north, along Interstate 95. As we drove on steadily at 70 miles per hour, I looked up to my nine o'clock position high and noticed the position lights and rotating beacon of an aircraft which seemed to be flying in a loose formation with us. I could not believe someone would be flying so slowly.

"Maybe he is going slow because it is really dark up there and he is just being careful," my wife joked. I was a little tired so it took me a moment to realize the poor Piper pilot or Cessna driver was bucking a major headwind. When I realized this, it made me think of *Joe's Maxim*. I have long said that if I am the pilot-in-command or the one responsible for paying the fuel bill, there will always be a headwind.

Now, it does not matter if I had just fought a headwind 500 miles to my destination. Just prior to take off on the return flight, there will be frontal passage and I will have the opportunity to enjoy another headwind on the return trip.

The problem with headwinds is that they keep you flying at lower altitudes where the air is more prone to turbulence. A pilot could climb higher into smoother air, but then has to pay the price of a higher headwind.

For the non-fliers reading this, it really is a process of simple math. Assume your airplane is capable of flying at 130 miles per hour. Unfortunately, there is a wind blowing directly in your face at 50 miles per hour. Consequently, your groundspeed will only be 80 miles per hour (130 − 50 = 80).

Occasionally, a pilot might "luck out." Those are the wonderful times in which you are up there cruising along at 130 miles per hour with a 50 mph tailwind (130 + 50 = 180).

Now, instead of plodding along at 80 mph, you can be zipping across the ground at three miles per minute. You may even be able to fly this in the smooth air at high altitude.

Thinking back on a lifetime of flying, two flights stand out as remarkably fast trips. One was in a jet, so you would expect it to be fast, the other was in my little Cessna.

The jet trip was at FL 240 with 0.72 M showing on the airspeed indicator. With a jet stream pushing us along with 180 knots on the tail, we were well over 750+ mph across the ground.

The Cessna flight came on a trip from Thomasville, GA back to Daytona Beach, FL. I was flying formation with another 170 and our trip to Daytona was phenomenally quick. We shaved almost 45 minutes off a normally two hour flight.

As I recall, those were my two good deals for the last 40 years.

Teaching Self-Confidence

Teaching student pilots to be confident aviators is one of the most challenging tasks facing a flight instructor. Older instructors have a better handle on this, while new CFIs may still be working on the concept.

What is confidence? Self-confidence begins with self-esteem and includes a component of knowledge. Part of self-confidence is judgment and yet another includes experience. All of these components make up what we describe as a confident pilot, one who exercises good judgment, and possesses good flying skills.

The issue for flight instructors becomes one of how to teach this confidence to their students. How do students acquire judgment? How do they obtain experience? Moreover, what do flight instructors have to be wary of in their students?

What makes a person a dangerous student pilot? Can a student be over confident? Which students would be prone to taking abnormal risks?

These are all very serious questions for a flight instructor, particularly a young and inexperienced CFI. If you are one of the latter, how would you deal with the over-confident, risk-taking student?

The key is training the student properly and setting the training environment by proper leadership. Performance in the airplane is dependent on a student's perceptions of his or her instructor's personal confidence. Then you have to work with each student individually.

When we talk of flight students, let's disregard their chronological age for a moment. There are those who are very experienced at a young age, and there are those who are older with no experience.

As flight instructors, we are the experienced. We are, if you will, the parents. It is our job to develop the student pilot into a well-rounded, highly motivated, and confident pilot. To this degree, our job is not unlike that of a parent.

Unfortunately, parents can do great harm to their children's developing self-esteem and self-confidence. In his book, *The Power of Self-Esteem*, Nathan Branden points out parents can hinder their child's growth and self-esteem in any of several ways. A parent can harm children by emphasizing the child's shortcomings, ridiculing or humiliating the child—especially in front of others—or telling the child, he or she is valueless, or their ideas are not important.

Now you can take this list by Branden and where it says, "parent," insert the term, "CFI" or "flight instructor." Likewise, where it says "children" or "child," use the term, "student pilot."

As instructors, essentially we are parents: treating the student pilots as children. And I don't mean in a condescending manner as you might treat a troublesome adolescent. In other words, we have to treat students as people for whom we truly care.

I have often told the student flight instructors I have helped develop that whenever you teach anyone to fly, the first thing you must do is to teach each one of them as though they were a blood relative.

There should be no difference in the way you would teach a person you don't know as compared to teaching your brother, sister, father, or mother. They should all get "the same treatment."

It is part of being a professional.

Negative Transfer

You can find one of the greatest examples of a negative transfer of learning in the cockpit of many of today's training aircraft. For whatever reason, some time ago the industry decided steering yokes were more desirable rather than control sticks.

For students who are learning to fly before they learn how to drive, the question of a negative transfer of learning is moot. However, for the vast majority of student pilots who learned how to drive first, using a control yoke in an airplane is, in many ways, opposite of how it would be used in a car.

When a student pilot begins learning to taxi an aircraft for the first time, their natural inclination is to try "driving" the airplane around the taxiways and runways. A flight instructor's best bet on keeping students from doing this begins on a day with calm winds, which would not require aileron inputs during the taxi. In this situation, the flight instructor can direct the student to literally sit on their left hand and use their right hand to control the throttle.

The negative transfer of learning is particularly enhanced and more critical during landing with a crosswind. Once the student lines up the runway with a crosswind from the left, the wind correction angle will be to the left; the student pilot knows the airplane must line up with the runway before touching down. In their mind, the way to move the airplane's nose to the right is by "steering" it.

This is, of course, exactly the wrong thing to do.

When the inexperienced pilot turns the "steering wheel" to the right to make the front of the airplane go to the right, naturally the left wing will rise up. As it does, the left crosswind gets underneath the left wing pushing it higher to cause an out of control situation.

If the student recognizes the situation quickly and has enough altitude, he or she may be able to avoid a serious accident. On the other hand, if this happens close to the ground, the downwind wheel (in this example, the right wheel) may dig into the runway. Depending on the strength of the wind and the speed of the aircraft, the plane may "skip" a couple of times or the right wing may very well dig into the ground spinning the airplane around.

The only way to properly train your student pilots to recognize this situation and avoid the associated hazards is by taking them out on a day with a fair and constant crosswind. To emphasize and reinforce the idea of using the rudder to align the aircraft with the runway and check the drift using aileron, they have to easily be able to see this condition for themselves. To do this, carefully have them fly the aircraft along the center line of a runway with a fairly strong and steady crosswind.

This exercise allows them to gain a sense of what it takes to keep the nose straight down the runway with rudder while keeping the airplane from drifting to the side with aileron.

After practicing a few of those one-wheel first crosswind landings and showing them how they must increase the control deflection as the airspeed decreases, they will soon become adept at landings in any condition. They will also naturally figure out the definition of negative transfer of learning.

If I could have my way, all primary training aircraft would be tailwheel airplanes equipped with control sticks instead of wheels.

What Makes a Really Good Pilot?

So, you want to be a good pilot. No, you want to be a *great* pilot. You want people to regard you as one of the best pilots with whom they have ever flown. Not too lofty a goal, is it? Or might it be?

What makes a really good pilot? Judgment is one aspect — never take a risk with someone onboard. Don't take risks solo, for that matter. You should also fly smoothly. This means checking the weather and flying passengers only when the weather is stable. You must also fly without any harsh or fast control inputs. Finally, you have to bring your passengers back to the ground safely in the event something, like an emergency, happens.

When I was a young and inexperienced pilot, I feared engine failures. Today, after more thousands of hours of experience and 40 years of flying, I regard them as an inconvenience at altitude, and something to be ready for on takeoff.

Most of the time an engine quits, it is the pilot's fault. Engines quit because the pilot allowed the airplane to run out of gas or they mismanaged the fuel by allowing a fuel tank to run dry.

There are rules you must follow when the engine quits. First, pitch to keep the proper airspeed; second, find a place to land; third, try to determine the cause of the failure; finally, if it does not restart, *safely land*. It truly is that simple.

Here is something else to go along with the procedure in the previous paragraph. Always have a place in mind to land in the event of an engine failure. In other words, the only time a pilot should be surprised by an engine failure, is on takeoff. Once the aircraft reaches a safe altitude, the pilot should constantly have a place to land, should the powerplant go silent. Once you have flown beyond that place, pick another safe landing area ahead. Then when you are beyond that one, you repeat the process until you arrive safely at your destination.

Keeping a place to land in mind as you fly is the first half of the battle. The second half includes putting the airplane down on the piece of turf you have decided to make into an emergency airport.

If your primary flight instructor told you to land "anywhere in the first third of the runway" during your simulated engine out practice, and then said that was acceptable, he lied to you. For instance, if you learned how to fly from a 3000 long runway, and your ability to land power-off is plus or minus 500 feet from a predetermined spot, you do not possess the skills to be successful in an actual emergency.

To land an airplane power-off effectively, you must have the skill to plan your approach and land within 50 feet of where you want to touch down. The reason for this is simple; if you lose your engine over inhospitable terrain and the only patch of land is about 700 feet long, you will have a difficult time landing the airplane safely if you are not capable of controlling your glide path, airspeed, and touchdown point.

The key is practice. You have to train yourself to understand the nuances of controlling airspeed and glide to arrive exactly where you want to go. After a little bit of practice, you'll be surprised at how closely you can land to your spot without power.

Okay, I will admit, engine failure on takeoff is still a little scary.

Adaptation

Sometimes life will throw you a curve and you have no choice other than to adapt. In the case of those who want to fly professionally, sometimes the curve ball is color blindness.

Color blindness is usually a problem for the male of the human species; females are carriers of the trait, but very rarely are they afflicted. Seven to 10 percent of all males suffer some degree of color blindness.

So, young person, there you are, preparing yourself for your flying career and you have already picked out the house of your dreams, the next five cars and two boats you plan to buy over the coming 10 or 15 years, your soul-mate and children. Now it appears as though you won't be able to get your "dream job."

Now what? How can you possibly afford all the toys you thought you were going to buy earlier in your life? And how will you pay for all your children and their toys?

It is time…to adapt.

Many times, most of the young people I work with fail to make the important connection between having a plan and having a backup plan. It is very similar to flying a cross-country flight; you have a destination, and you should have your alternate destination —just in case the weather goes down or another problem befalls the destination airport.

At their young age, most new pilots lack the vision required to look "over the horizon." I know this because when I was that age, I also lacked "over the horizon vision." Most young adults have not really lived enough to understand "the big picture." Many times, all they see is what they want to see and not what is really there, right in front of them, which is theirs for the taking.

Another way to view this is to understand flying big jets is not the only way in life to make a living. You can find other means to collect a paycheck. The real trick is to discover something else as exciting as flying big iron.

I have counseled numerous young pilots who have just discovered they are color blind. Many believe their flying days are over. This simply is not the case; in many instances, they can fly, just maybe not as a commercial pilot. Various degrees of color blindness may still allow an individual to fly, it just may require a waiver for private or personal operation of aircraft. For these individuals, I say start a business, make a lot of money, and fly around in your own company jet.

Here's the secret: be productive. Create, serve, connect. Use your business to help others make a living. You will thoroughly enjoy the sense of well-being this creates for both those you help and yourself.

Oh, one other thing. Do something you really like and it will seem as though you never work.

Have fun, be happy.

The High Cost of Renting

In 1971, the cost of renting airplanes was expensive. The sad truth about aircraft rental today is that it still remains prohibitively expensive. Relatively speaking, it is more expensive today than 40 - 45 years ago. In 1971, a Cessna 150 cost $15 per hour. Divided by the minimum wage at that time of $1.60, the exchange was 9.4 hours of work per hour of flight. Today the very same Cessna 150, now old and tired, rents for about $80 per hour. At today's minimum wage of $7.25, that equals 11.0 work hours per flight hour. This begs the question of how in the world can young people afford flight training?

Assuming the average private pilot spends 30 hours dual and 25 hours solo at $109 dual and $80 solo respectively, students will pay $5,270 in rental and instructional fees. Tacked onto this will follow other charges for ground instruction, textbooks, navigation plotters, computers, testing fees, and the bill for the checkride. In all, the final cost for earning a private pilot certificate can easily exceed $6000 or $7000, sometimes more than $10,000, and as much as $15,000.

Six or seven thousand dollars is a lot of money. Young people, especially those with dreams right out of high school, don't have that kind of money. Consequently, they spend their money on things more within their grasp, putting off flying lessons until later. Sometimes an entire lifetime; sometimes forever. And who suffers? They do — and so do those of us in the aviation industry. Eventually, the flying public will also suffer — airlines have already canceled flights for lack of aircrew.

In aviation training today, dual rates average $95 to $150 per hour or more. Students have grumbled about the high cost of flight training while assuming flight instructors and flight school owners are getting rich. Unfortunately, as those of us in the business know, this is simply not the case.

While it would seem flight school operators enjoy a high degree of profit, in most cases this is untrue. Those who reap the rewards of high rental rates are the gas companies, parts manufacturers, insurance carriers, and local governments. Oh, by the way, those rewards are relatively small. In short, everyone is profiting from the high costs, except the owner of the flight school. Most of the time, like all other small business owners, they are the last to take their paycheck while trying to pay their employees and keep their business going.

Assuming a small flight school has five aircraft and a small operation at a municipal airport, the numbers might stack up something like this for an operation flying 2500 hours per year:

	Annually	Monthly	Hourly
Payment on the airplanes	$27,000	$2,250	$10.80
Lease on office space	$18,000	$1,500	$7.20
Utilities	$4,800	$400	$1.92
Salaries for 3 employees	$90,000	$7,500	$36.00
Taxes for 3 employees	$16,200	$1,350	$6.48
Benefits for 3 employees	$22,500	$1,875	$9.00
Insurance	$12,500	$1,042	$5.00
Fuel	$66,500	$5,542	$26.60
Oil	$3,125	$260	$1.25
Inspections/maintenance	$22,375	$1,865	$8.95
Total	$283,000	$23,583	$113.20

This is a rather conservative estimate. As you can see, the cost of operation is at $113.20 per hour for the aircraft. That's cost. Tack on 15 percent for profit—again, a rather conservative estimate—and the rental rate comes out to be $130 per hour. At a 15 percent markup, the owner of the flight school only nets about $42,450. After taxes, take home is about $30,000.

No one is getting rich at that rate.

The Mystery of Lift

In science writer-editor Jules Bergman's book, *Anyone Can Fly*, he opens with a story of asking a little boy why airplanes fly. The child explains, in essence, that airplanes float on the air.

I like that—because it is so simple—and almost true.

When I ask the same question of older students, some reply with a somewhat similar answer, only with a little more sophistication. Then I slam them with the truth. Sometimes they have a little trouble handling the truth, like the famous line delivered by Colonel Nathan R. Jessep played by Jack Nicholson in the movie, "A Few Good Men."

"The truth? You can't handle the truth!"

The truth, in this case, involves a little math. Basically, lift equals $1/2$ rho times velocity squared times the coefficient of lift times the wing area ($L = 1/2$ r V^2 Cl S).

In math, the equation (in parentheses, above) is somewhat intimidating. Less so written in English, as in the first part of the paragraph. However, it remains intimidating to the majority of flight students. But the words and the equation should not be scary at all. It is simpler than one can imagine. The equation can be further reduced down to a very simple explanation.

First, there is nothing that can be done about rho, air density. So let's throw that out of the equation. (If you're really curious, rho is .002377 slugs per cubic foot at sea level in standard conditions.) The other factor a pilot has no control over is the wing area. We will assume for cruise, we cannot adjust the wing area in flight. For landing, once the flaps are full down, again, wing area remains constant.

So, what this boils our equation down to is this: $L = V \times Cl$. In English, this means Lift equals Speed times Angle-of-attack (AoA).

Now, to what kind of practical application can we put this information?

Well, if we are cruising, we know that if we speed up, the airplane will climb. If we slow down, we are going to lose altitude. Another thing we know is that if we keep the airspeed constant by not varying the power, by increasing the AoA by pulling back on the yoke, we will climb. Conversely, pushing the yoke forward and decreasing our AoA will cause us to lose altitude.

These four things, altitude, power, pitch, and airspeed, are interrelated. Pilots must understand the relationship between all four very well. You must also have knowledge of where you are on the power curve. Either you are on the "front side" or on the "back side" and your position on the curve has everything to do with how you operate the flight controls.

Understanding the lift equation is particularly important for executing short field landings. Maintaining the correct glide path and airspeed for a precise touchdown is extremely difficult if you fail to understand the equation. It is much easier if you do.

More on the short field landing to follow.

-30-

The Short Field Landing

Now, let's talk about some of the secrets to the short field landing. We'll also discuss how the lift equation plays so importantly in "making the point."

One of the most challenging and fun things in flying is the short field landing. I like it because, well, I like landing on short fields. There is no more boring place to land than at an "airport" with long concrete runways. Country airports with short, grass runways are so much more interesting and fun. For the prospective pilots who really want the greatest challenge, fly jets in the Navy where the runway is not only short, but moves up and down and left and right as you approach to land.

When it comes to landing on a short field, it is important to land right on the end of the runway. You cannot afford "float" and you cannot land short. There is no option when it comes to touchdown; it has to be on the spot. Additionally, you have to arrive at the spot right at stall speed.

The question is, how do you get the airplane on the spot at stall?

The first thing you have to know is where to aim. There are pilots who say aim short of the touchdown point. This is wrong on so many levels! Pilots who aim short of their touchdown point and flight instructors who teach that technique are using speed as a crutch.

If you are aiming short of your touchdown point, don't be surprised if one day you end up landing short of the runway. This is okay if the area short of the runway is grass and you can roll downward onto the runway. However, if there is a lip to the concrete, you will leave your landing gear at the end of the runway on the lip, while the aircraft continues down the runway sans wheels.

You have to remember what your driver's ed coach told you about skidding on a wet or icy road. "Don't look at the telephone pole!" They teach this because wherever the driver's eyes are looking, that is where the car will go.

The same holds true in landing an airplane. When you are looking short of your point, the airplane will go to that point. If you fly beyond your aim point, it is because you are flying the approach too fast or your transition is improper, resulting in "float."

As I previously mentioned in explaining the lift equation, the math can be reduced to the concept that lift equals speed times angle-of-attack (L = S x AoA).

The lift required for any airspeed or glide path is dependent on AoA. For instance, for straight and level, if the airplane weighs 2400 pounds, you can say the airplane is flying at 105 knots with 22.6 units of AoA. If the airplane stalls at 42 knots, the stalling AoA is 57.1 units. (Again, we have simplified the equation, disregarding the factors of rho and wing area.)

For an airplane flown on a short field approach, we assume a short field approach speed of 60 knots. This means the angle-of-attack will be 40 units AoA. Keep in mind power is the element that actually determines the glide path. The more power used, the shallower the approach path. For a steep approach, you would use idle power; for straight and level at slow flight, the power setting will be higher.

For an approach and landing on a short field, we would use a reduced power setting for a steeper approach, we maintain the airspeed at 60 knots and we have the airplane trimmed to 40 units AoA. As long as the pilot maintain this condition with the power set for the appropriate glide path, we will continue down the proper descent angle as we approach our aim point.

If we do not adjust power, but increase the AoA by pulling back on the yoke, the airplane will climb. In the same manner, if we reduce the power and maintain both airspeed and AoA, the airplane's descent path becomes steeper.

Now, here is the trick for aiming at the point and touching down exactly where you are aiming.

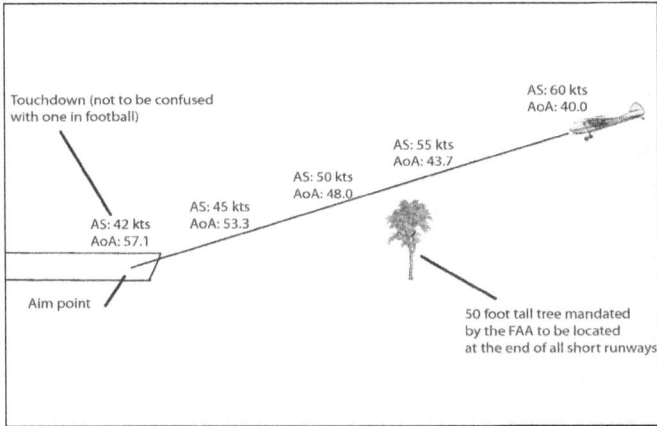

The Short Field Approach

When you are approaching the touchdown point, you have to coordinate the reduction of power with the increase of AoA to maintain the glide path. While approaching and preparing for the touchdown, you begin reducing the power and increasing pitch so that as airspeed decays, you maintain a combination of speed and AoA to keep the proper amount of force to sustain the glide path.

If the pilot performs the coordination of speed and AoA correctly, he or she will reach the touchdown point with an airspeed of 42 knots (stall speed) and an AoA of 57.1 units AoA (stalling AoA). Oh, and by the way, there is no float because the wing has arrived at the runway at stall. So what makes the short field approach a little more challenging?

Varying and gusting wind, of course.

The Soft Field Landing

I gave my insights to the short field landing previously; now it is time to discuss the soft field landing. As with the short field landing, many pilots today have little or no experience on an actual soft field. It is quickly becoming a long forgotten art, that of landing on grass runways.

Sometimes I am amused when I visit a large metropolitan airport and wander around talking with the local pilots, students, and instructors alike about flying. Flight schools located on former military bases, or at airports also serving the airlines, typically have hard surface runways longer than 6000 feet. Consequently, the students (and many of the younger instructors) rarely have had a chance actually to fly to or from a short or soft runway. Additionally, many insurance companies now forbid grass-field operations.

A soft surface is anything that is not paved. This includes grass runways, dirt strips, and muddy or snow-covered fields.

In talking to low time pilots about how they would fly into a soft field, when asked to describe exactly what they would do, they

A Cessna 170 departing a "soft" runway

are usually very good about reciting the procedures for the aircraft combined with the Practical Test Standards (PTS). What they lack is practical experience.

Here is the ugly truth about today's pilots and soft field landings: without working from an actual soft field with an experienced flight instructor, they will not get that practical experience. I am concerned for the newly rated pilot who makes his or her first actual soft field landing solo using the techniques described in textbooks and the PTS.

Without having really seen or practiced a landing on an authentic soft field, all bets are off regarding successful completion of the maneuver. Likely, it will all work out in the end and they will learn so much from that first, genuine dose, of practical experience. It is, however, so much easier to take the student out to a grass runway and practicing a few landings in the real environment before they are out on their own.

Many younger pilots are surprised to learn of my technique. When I tell them it usually takes two or three passes for me to get an airplane into an actual unknown soft strip, they ask why.

My first pass at a strip where I have never landed, I explain, is a low pass a couple of hundred feet above the landing surface to "check out" the landing area. I maintain a good airspeed—not too fast and certainly not too slow. I fly "downsun" from the strip so that if there is any standing water hidden by the grass, the sun will reflect off of it, letting me know it is there.

The second pass I fly, I will bring the airplane to the surface and "test" the runway. You can think of this as a modified touch and go, if you will, where I fly the airplane in slow flight at the surface. I keep aerodynamic control over the airplane with the weight completely supported by the wings while I let the wheels touch, "testing" the surface. If it feels too mushy, I will go somewhere else; if it is okay, and there remains enough runway to stop safely, I may land on that pass.

If there is not enough runway remaining to stop the airplane safely on the second pass, I will come around and set up for the third and final pass to the landing.

The key to all of this is slow flight. The whole point is to fly the airplane close enough to the ground to evaluate on the first pass, then on the ground to evaluate the surface on the second, and finally, the last pass is for the landing.

This is what real flying is all about: soft and short runways at non-towered country airports. Try it, I promise you will like it.

The Perfect Storm

We are facing a situation in the aviation industry, which many may very well describe as an approaching "Perfect Storm." For years, we have heard people in and out of the industry say there will be a pilot shortage. Current pilots, in search of their first jobs or those seeking better positions, have been asking, "So..., where is this pilot shortage?"

Observers within the industry, outside of the industry, and in government believe the pilot shortage is very real. From various sources, many report problems are approaching the aviation field over the next couple of decades.

In the past, there have been questions revolving around this idea of a pilot shortage. At first, it was coming with the retirement of the World War II pilots; then the Korean era pilots; now, with the Vietnam vets departing the cockpits, we are hearing of the shortage again. This time, there are aspects of this prediction completely different from the past. For one, the world's population is growing exponentially. Another factor is the addition of 30,000 more aircraft into the equation.

According to studies by Boeing, this Perfect Storm will create a shortfall of 466,650 pilots worldwide with as many as 97,350 in North America alone. These are big numbers. Additionally, as Captain Domenic Di Irio points out in a CBS interview, aviation training is expensive and many have chosen to pursue other career interests. This fact alone will have an incredible impact on the number of new pilots entering aviation. For those who already hold commercial certificates with instrument and multi-engines ratings, you are almost as good as hired. We have already seen flight cancellations due to a lack of cockpit flight crew.

Essentially, we are looking at a situation that many predicted before that did not happen as industry analysts foretold. Now many are skeptical. This is akin to the little boy crying wolf.

It now becomes a question of what young pilots today want to believe. Is the industry crying wolf, one more time, or is the industry going to become really "unglued" in a way no one ever predicted? What is required of today's young pilots is, as always, perseverance.

One of the saddest things I have seen in the past is a promising young pilot making the decision to leave aviation, only to suddenly see a surge in hiring. And because the young pilot has quit and gone on to work in another field, they were in essence, no longer in queue for a hiring position with the airlines. When they realized their mistake, by the time they were up to speed again after renting airplanes or flight instructing to get back on the step again, it was too late. The hiring boom had passed.

As with any endeavor, the key in this business is always to remain ready. Unfortunately, it takes great perseverance and sacrifice to stay positioned for the airlines; flight instruction is the best way to show continual and steady flying.

This, too, requires extreme dedication.

It boils down to the question of, "What do you really want to do with your life?"

If you want to be the captain of an airliner, you must stay the course until you get there. It might come earlier than you think. It might also come later.

However, you will never make it to the left seat if you quit.

A Near Miss

My students look at me with great incredulity. "No way!" one says. "Six inches?"

"Yep. At least we think it was six inches. It might have been closer."

"How could you measure a miss that close?" another asks.

"Simple. We moved the airplanes to the closest point we could estimate when they passed and then put the prop of the Ercoupe vertical. There was about five and a half inches between the top of the prop arc and the bottom of my wing," I explained. Then I went on, as Paul Harvey would say, to tell the rest of the story.

We were headed to the Tampa Bay area for a fly-in of our antique airplane aviation group. The little grass field where we landed had a road paralleling the runway. The local hosts parked us in a line with our tails to the road, about 30 airplanes in all parked wingtip-to-wingtip.

Most of my friends had acquired hotel rooms or set up tents for the evening. Since I grew up in Tampa and my best friend still lived there, I decided to fly over to an airport north of Tampa at about 10 p.m. — Paul was still working until after 11 p.m.

I went out to my Cessna 170, pre-flighted, climbed in, and fired up the engine. Since the tail faced the road and there was no traffic and there was a pasture on the other side of the road, I did a quick engine run-up in the spot. Then I taxied out to Runway 9. After my departure call, I applied full power and began rolling.

The night was dark. Real dark.

At about the time I my tail lifted off the ground, I saw the Ercoupe. It was right in the middle of the runway without any lights. The silver airframe appeared as a ghostly figure in the beam of my landing light.

The prop arc of the Ercoupe passed about 6 to 12 inches outboard of where the strut joined the wing on my Cessna. I instinctively threw in full right aileron to try lifting the left wing. I went by the Ercoupe while looking at it to confirm the lights were out. They were.

I lost my sense of direction on the dark runway. I knew fences bordered each side of the runway. I had to fly and fly now!

I reached down and grabbed the flap handle. I snatched on 20 degrees of flaps; I was very happy for manual flaps—there's nothing better than being able to get half flaps instantly.

I didn't know where the needle was pointing on the airspeed indicator; I was flying the airplane by feel. After I knew I was airborne and clear of the fence, I felt compelled to look over my shoulder at the Ercoupe once more. I had to make sure I was right about the Ercoupe's lights being off. They were. As I looked at the dark apparition sitting in the middle of the runway, the nav lights suddenly popped on.

I circled overhead to pull my heart out of my throat and the seat cushion out of my... Down below, a couple of my friends were watching. They had witnessed the whole event.

Later, they would tell me both the Ercoupe pilot and I yelled "Clear!" at the same moment. Neither of us heard the other and then we stared our respective airplanes simultaneously, so again, we did not hear one another.

After I settled down, I landed to have a little "debriefing" with the Ercoupe pilot. I asked him why he was moving an airplane around in the dark without lights. I also asked if he was aware of the regulatory requirement of turning on nav lights when moving airplanes in the dark.

Months later, he told me "the rest of the story." As he was moving across the runway, his nosewheel fell into a "gopher hole," causing him to stop. Then he had to work the nosewheel of the airplane out of the hole very carefully.

"Had I not fallen into the hole," he said, "More than likely, we would have hit prop-to- prop."

Yes, we were very lucky that night.

Intro to Instrument Flying

When I was a young and most inexperienced private pilot with all of about 100 hours, I had the opportunity to participate in an instrument flight flown by a classmate from college. It was an interesting, and enlightening, flight.

At the time Gary had about 230 flights hours and his instrument rating could not be any fresher. Since he had about twice my flight time and held an instrument rating, this made him the most experienced pilot in our peer group.

Still, all of us in our little group were inexperienced and really didn't know what we were doing. Oh, the blissful unawareness of the uneducated ignorant!

It was a typical spring day for Florida. This translates into weak cold front pushing through to the south with the attendant problems of inclement weather—replete with the probable thunderstorms.

And of course, we ended up in the middle of one of the storms.

At the time I was, at my level of experience, uhmm... how can I say this...? Totally clueless.

We were being slammed around the inside of a huge cumulonimbus cloud and I did not like it one bit. But hey! I was learning and wasn't this what I was going to do as a career for the rest of my life? Time to man-up.

Of course, we could not see anything beyond the cockpit. I was keeping watchful eye on the attitude indicator and Gary seemed to be doing a credible job keeping the wings level. We were bouncing around a bit, but Gary seemed to have it all under control.

Until all hell broke loose.

Suddenly, the clouds slammed us up and down with the appropriate excursions in bank. Gary was on the radio with Miami Center trying to find a way out of the mess.

Center was vectoring us around and Gary was flying the airplane, trying to find Victor airways and intersections on the chart, and talking on the radio. In the meantime, we're bouncing off the overhead, bulkheads, and door.

Now it was getting dark. Oh, no, the sun was full up. It was just dark inside the cloud.

It was about this time *The Thought* struck me: I can't do this! Gary was sitting in the left seat barely hanging on. He had a lot more experience than I did. I would never be able to do what he was doing!

I actually began thinking I needed to consider other career fields.

At about the darkest moment, we broke out into daylight and clear air. Things settled down in the cockpit. I decided to wait on the idea of other career choices.

I'm glad I did.

I may have been intimidated that day more than 40 years ago. But I learned later that as with anything in life, earning an instrument rating is something you accomplish one day at a time.

You have to learn to crawl before you walk; then you must learn to walk fast. Then jog. After that, comes running.

Then one day, you find you have no trouble at all sprinting.

Dave, You're Working Too Hard!

I read with interest the insights learned by an Australian friend, Dave, a middle-aged (as he refers to himself) young person who is learning how to fly. For his insight #13, he wrote on his blog, "Watch the airspeed on late finals! I made one really slow landing on which I was going as low as 50 knots even before I was over the runway threshold. That's too close to the stall (even though I had full flaps out). Need to maintain about 65 knots over the airport fence and 60 knots over the runway threshold."

Dave, you're working too hard! Sit back and relax! Enjoy it! Trim the airplane and let her do most of the work.

One of the simplest things a pilot can do to help in flying the airplane, particularly during landing, is to trim properly for the correct airspeed. I have sat in airplanes many times as a check pilot or instructor watching students struggle with slow flight. They sit in the left seat working really hard to keep the airplane right on altitude, right on airspeed.

Watching the student pilots struggle, I remember back to the time when I did the same. It seems we all fight with the concept of flying slow. Combine that with the fear of stalls and falling out of the sky and merge the idea of flying an approach close to the ground and you have the equation for an impediment to learning.

Dave, keep in mind that once you get the airplane properly established on the glideslope at a particular approach speed, if you trim the airplane correctly, it will arrive at the landing area with only small inputs from you. It also will stay right on speed because you *trimmed* her for *that* speed.

All that remains after reaching the runway is to reduce the power and ease her nose up into the stalled condition—right at the correct moment and height. The wing should quit flying and the wheels should start rolling all at the same time. If you manage that, the landing will be smooth with hardly a bump at touchdown.

Then the trick is to keep the stick (wheel, yoke, or elevator control) full aft as you roll out while at the same time, programming the ailerons into the wind if there is a crosswind.

And there it is! No sweat! A perfect landing!

Oh, yeah, I forgot to mention you have to use your feet to keep it going straight down the middle of the landing area, or on the centerline of the runway.

Fly well, learn a lot, be safe.

Teaching Straight and Level

One of the first things a student pilot needs to learn is the task of flying straight and level. Sounds simple enough, right? It is, to a degree. Still, there are elements of performing the maneuver (can straight and level be considered a maneuver?) every pilot should master.

Breaking the maneuver down to the simplest elements is the first thing a flight instructor should accomplish. Then the CFI should present the information so the student can understand the basics of flying the airplane in a straight line at a level altitude.

The instructor must first address the issue of the student's individual sitting height in the airplane. Every student is going to have a different visual perspective once seated in the airplane. This means when the student is sitting in the pilot's seat, he or she will have a particular "sight picture" looking over the nose of the airplane. In other words, a short student might have very little clearance between the top of the cowling and the horizon while a tall student might look out the front and have an apparent view of four of five inches distance between the cowling and the horizon.

This apparent sight picture is important for the student to visualize in order to keep the airplane from climbing or descending while flying straight ahead. With any given power setting, the airplane will maintain altitude at a specific airspeed. For example, with 2400 rpm set in a Cessna 150, the airplane may be capable of 98 knots indicated airspeed. If the pilot pitches up too high, the airplane will slow down and climb. Pitched too low, it will descend and increase speed.

If the pilot wants to maintain altitude and reduce power, the student pilot will have to pitch the nose up slightly. Similarly, if the pilot pushes the throttle all the way forward, he or she must decrease the nose attitude to maintain constant altitude. This, of course, directly relates to the idea of the angle-of-attack (AoA) changing for particular power settings. The slower a pilot flies, the higher AoA is required to produce the same amount of lift. The higher the AoA, the higher the apparent nose position while flying in level flight.

Regarding the direction of flight, flight instructors should avoid the temptation to say, "Hold your heading steady." Many students have little concept of what that exactly means.

It is easier to explain that as long as the wings are level, the airplane will travel a straight line. It is even better to look out the front of the airplane and say, "See that lake over there? Fly the airplane directly to it."

It will take little time for the student to master the maneuver of straight and level. From there, they can go on to learn about the other three areas of the four fundamentals, which include climbs, descents, and turns.

Teaching Stalls, Part I

One maneuver scary to many student pilots is *The Stall*. This maneuver comes in a variety of flavors — there is the power off stall, the power on stall, the approach to landing stall, the accelerated stall. It is no surprise this is scary for new pilots.

When we talk of "stalls" with the initiates, we must take care to explain it has nothing to do with the failure of the engine. So many inexperienced pilots believe when a flight instructor or another pilot mentions the term, "stall," it has something to do with engine failure. Keep in mind engines "quit," wings "stall."

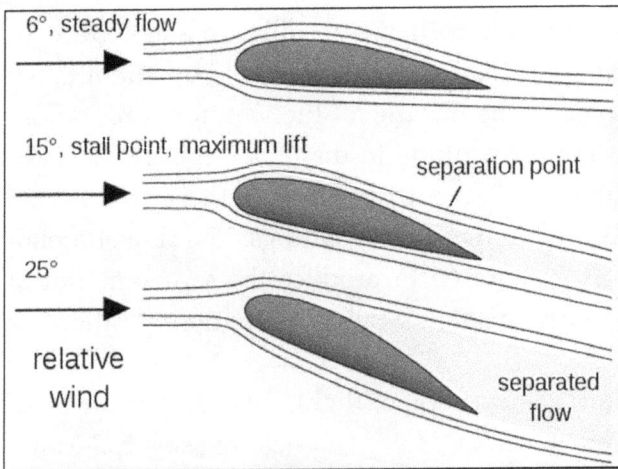

The Stall

Engine failure is a completely different topic I will talk about in other areas of the book, but for now, new pilots or would-be pilots need to know when experienced pilots talk about stalls, it has to do with the wing's ability to produce lift. It has nothing to do with the engine.

When we speak of a wing stalling, we are referring to the smooth airflow of the relative wind across the top and bottom of the wing. The wing has to "cut" through the air with what we call an "angle-of-attack" (AoA). This angle is relatively small in order for the wing to produce the lift required to fly. If the pilot increases the AoA, the wing begins cutting through the air too greatly, disrupting the airflow over the top of the wing.

Should this happen, the wing "stalls" and can no longer lift the airplane into the sky. Now don't be alarmed, this sounds worse than it actually is — at the moment the stall happens, the airplane quits flying and begins "falling out of the sky." OK, that, too, sounds bad, but it is not.

While falling out of the sky seems terrible to the uninitiated, it really is not. Here is something you have to keep in mind: when the wing is stalled, it can instantly be "unstalled" (properly referred to as "recovered") simply by releasing the "backpressure" on the stick, yoke, or wheel on which you are pulling.

The moment you release the stick, the elevators come down which allows the nose to lower, decreasing the AoA. This *immediately* starts the wing flying again.

Now, for the technical terms — the angle of the wing as it slices through the air is known as the angle-of-attack or AoA as noted above; the wind the airplane is flying through by passing over and under the wing is known as the relative wind; the angle of the nose relative to the horizon is the pitch attitude; and the speed of the relative wind passing the aircraft is airspeed.

For the flight instructors out there teaching, this is really one of the most important points to keep in mind. When you introduce stalls to your student, you need to do so slowly and gently... What do I mean?

For one, allow your student to realize the stall and stall recovery has nothing to do with the engine. You can do this by introducing power off stalls with recovery simply by controlling the AoA. Few instructors do this because all the books refer to "applying full power to minimize the loss of altitude on the recovery." This in itself is a scary phrase for a new pilot to read or hear. However, let me ask you this: does a glider pilot apply full power on stall recovery?

No, of course not. Sailplane pilots simply lower the nose (decreasing the AoA) to get the glider flying again. It has nothing to do with engine power. This is something you should introduce to your students at the beginning of training. This alone allows the student to associate the importance of decreasing the AoA to get the aircraft flying again.

Another thing to focus on is the kinesthetic. Students have to understand there is no extreme dropping off, or falling out of control, or anything that scary. One thing I do to help explain and demonstrate to students that the pilot is in full control of the airplane, is to go to a relatively high altitude, reduce power to idle, and stall the airplane's wing. Then I will sit there with the stick full back keeping the wings level with the use of rudder. As we come down, I release the backpressure, or pitch, and the airplane starts flying immediately. Then I slowly pull the nose up again into another stall.

The student quickly realizes you can still control the airplane regardless of what is happening with the wing. In other words, you can control the AoA of the wing and choose when it flies and when you want it stalled.

Flying is, of course, all about control.

Teaching Stalls, Part II

First, some important questions. Why should we learn how to stall? Why should we learn how to recover from a stall? What is the importance of stalls? When do stalls occur? Can we minimize the loss of altitude when we stall? At what speeds can stalls occur? Does stall speed change? Are Rin-Tin-Tin and Lassie friends?

Aw, okay, the last one actually has nothing to do with stalls. I was just wondering...

Let's take a look at the first question posed above: why should we learn about stalls? As with anything in aviation, we need to know. More importantly, our minds and muscles need to know. Sometimes the onset of a stalled condition is very subtle; as pilots, we need to know when the wing has actually stopped flying so we can initiate recovery procedures. This might allow us to avoid contacting the ground in a way we would prefer to avoid.

Now, for the follow-on question of why we need to learn recovery techniques: after being able to recognize when the stall has happened, we also need to be able to tell when the wing is flying again. We should be confident in the recovery procedures and also be able to understand and as well as know when the wing is actually producing lift.

Now for the third question: what is the importance of stalls? For one, when we land the airplane, we need to get the craft as slow as possible as we come down to the landing area. Ideally, we want the wing to quit flying the moment the wheels touch down. In order to accomplish this, we must fully understand the procedure of stalling. We also need to know how to perform the maneuver safely, as well as recognize that it has happened.

Yes, you can land an airplane without stalling, but not on a bona fide short field. Any excess speed at the time of touch down has an exponential effect on the distance of the landing rollout.

So, controlling airspeed on final approach is the core of the stall and speed relationship. Another way of looking at this is to understand that in order to be safe, the pilot needs to be capable of flying with confidence at any airspeed and avoid becoming too slow on final.

The problem with getting too slow on final is the inadvertent stall so very close to the ground. If this happens, there may not be enough altitude to recover the airplane before hitting the ground out of control.

As a pilot, especially if flying into a relatively short runway, you have to fly with confidence. The only way you can do this is by practicing stalls and stall recoveries and feeling comfortable in knowing the warnings of impending stall.

Regarding the question of when, and at what airspeed stalls can occur, I talked about this earlier (see Any Attitude, Any Airspeed, page 79). As a student pilot, you will probably hear your flight instructor reciting the mantra: "Stalls can happen at any altitude, any airspeed, and any attitude."

It is true. Stalls can happen anytime, anywhere, at any speed— if you allow it. The trick to minimizing the loss of altitude is recognizing the stall as it happens and recovering right away. An attentive pilot can recover most airplanes with very little loss of altitude.

As for Rin-Tin-Tin and Lassie being friends, the question really begs the answer as to how old you really are. If you know who Rin-Tin-Tin and Lassie are, well, you're kind of old...

The Almost Did Club

The old pilots, those much older (and presumably wiser) than me, have proclaimed, "There are those who have and those who will." What they are referring to are pilots who *have* landed an airplane gear up and pilots who *will* land gear up. Personally, I think there is a group of pilots in the middle. And I belong to that group—"The Almost Did's."

One has to ask how a pilot could possibly land an airplane gear up today with all the redundant backup warning systems. To this, I give the junior officer's hand salute (palms up shrug).

In my case, on the night in question when I joined The Almost Did's, I was breaking the rules. I was breaking my rules. I was tired and should not have been flying. But the company was short of pilots, I was young, and I was a "hacker," someone who could do anything.

This event happened when I was a charter pilot flying checks at night for a now defunct company. I typically flew five to eight hours a night spread over a 12-hour period. My route started at 9 p.m. and finished at 9 a.m. and I would sleep all day and get up to fly again all night. It was a romantic, hard, time. There is nothing like flying all night, if you can stay awake and feel rested enough to be safe about it.

Which was possible, if you slept all day.

But this one day, the company called me at 1 p.m., right in the middle of my sleep cycle. They wanted redundant information on the gripe I had written on the plane after the previous night's flying.

I was never able to go back to sleep.

I should have said, "I'm not flying tonight." What I did was crawl into the airplane and depart Tampa International for Orlando International. There I was in my trusty 210 and I found myself working on autopilot along with the airplane. What happened next has stayed with me for an entire career.

Automaticity had taken over. For those of you who don't know the definition of that fancy word, automaticity is what keeps you going when you are too tired to keep going. You experience it as the event of getting home after a long, tiring day and night, but you don't remember driving your car home, you don't remember the red lights, you cannot remember leaving your departure point. It just happens.

In my case, that night I was in the middle of the landing flare when I had the sudden thoughts, *I don't remember talking to tower; I don't remember lowering the landing gear; I don't remember extending the flaps.*

I don't remember doing the GUMP check! (Gas, Undercarriage, Mixtures Rich, Props Forward.)

I uttered that famous four-letter expletive-deleted usually uttered just before an airplane crash. At the same time, I crammed the throttle into the firewall. Simultaneously, the tires screeched on the runway prompting me to yank the power to idle again, but the excess energy already transferred to the airframe and we went bouncing horribly up and down runway 18L. It had to be the worst landing of my life.

As the airplane settled down, I literally looked over toward the staging area and uttered, "I hope no one saw that!"

Ever since, I GUMP on gear extension, turning base, and then again on short final, regardless of the airplane I am flying. I also make sure I remember it.

And I no longer fly when I am tired.

Flying at (Density) Altitude

I am a Florida boy who learned to fly at mean sea level. As such, I do not care for a couple of things. The first is cold, the second is high density altitude.

Many pilots do not understand the concept of density altitude (DA). When the temperature is high, particularly at higher pressure altitudes, the DA is increased. When DA increases, there is less air for the airplane and the engine to work with to fly. In other words, you lose a lot of performance capability.

Inexperienced pilots do not know what this means when it comes to taking off or landing. Sometimes they completely underestimate what high DA does to their climb capability. This is across the board, for all airplanes.

For instance, when I was a younger pilot flying A-7s, my first encounter with high DA took place at NAS Fallon, NV. I was thankful for a thorough brief by the more experienced fleet pilots, which prepared us "new guys" for the first landing at an elevation of 3,934 feet MSL with an OAT of 109 degrees F. I will never forget how much more energy the jet had at touchdown—all with normal parameters; I can remember sitting in the cockpit muttering, "Whoa, Big Fella!" as the Corsair blew past the nine board on a 14,000 foot long runway with great speed. That experience did not hold a candle to taking off in my Cessna 170, months later at Truckee Tahoe.

I was flying around with a couple of other Naval officers in the 170. We went over to TRK for an airshow. When we were on downwind, a pilot flying a Mig 15 for the show treated us to a long and hot landing. As a result, he ran off the end of the runway. Luckily, no one was hurt and there was only minimal damage to the Mig.

The show was great and it was time to leave. I figured take off gross weight was somewhere in the range of about 2140 pounds, about 60 pounds shy of Cessna 170's gross weight. I looked at the performance charts calculating all I needed to know. And what I needed to know was a bit. . . illuminating.

Takeoff distance was incredibly long and the initial climb rate was less than 200 fpm. When it was out time to go, I pulled onto the runway, ran up the engine to full power, and started leaning. I tweaked the mixture until I had the highest rpm out of the engine and released the brakes.

Now, down here in "normal life" at MSL, the airplane typically lurches down the runway. Up at TRK with a DA of about 9000 feet, she just sat there. In my mind's eye, I could almost see her head turning around like one of the cartoon planes in Disney's movie and asking, "Really?"

After she protested some, she started rolling forward, ever so slowly. I felt as though I had enough time to read the latest Trade-A-Plane before reaching rotation. Finally, there was enough airspeed to get the tail off the ground and eventually, we had enough to liftoff.

The climb rate was in fact, measly. The VSI needle settled at slightly less than 200 fpm. Fortunately, takeoff was off to the north into somewhat flat terrain.

Yeah, I am a Florida boy who likes the lower DA of MSL. But I also really liked the scenery of the mountains. If you ever have the chance to fly out west in the Sierra Nevadas, the Rockies, or elsewhere, take it. The flying is spectacular.

Just be careful and pay very close attention to all the information from your performance charts.

Leftovers

Leftovers. You have to love 'em. Especially if they have been hanging around the 'fridge for a while and they age appropriately — mixing flavors in on top of other flavors. Sometimes the leftovers are wonderfully tasty and you might think it cannot be better.

Or can it?

For aviators, there might be something more wonderful than leftovers in the refrigerator. What could a pilot use more than—? Gas. And not the kind that irritates one's stomach — we're talking about real gas, the kind of stuff that keeps airplanes in the air. Liquid gold, 80- and 100-octane, maybe 100-LL, and for some, jet fuel.

No matter the type of fuel in the tanks and running through the engines, you have to keep in mind there is a legal amount you must have in the tanks when you shut down after landing. The FAA says it is 30 minutes at normal cruise power settings for day VFR flights and 45 minutes for night flights or IFR operations.

Thirty minutes flying time is not much. Forty-five minutes isn't that much more.

If you have flown an airplane down to these fuel levels, you know how nerve-wracking it can be; if it does not make you nervous, perhaps you are not paying enough attention. Keep in mind that a dwindling fuel supply may hamper any pilot's critical thinking skills.

Many pilots agree these fuel reserves are too low. A Piper Cherokee or Cessna 172 powered by a 150-hp Lycoming with a nominal fuel flow of 8 gph can land from a night or IFR flight with only 6 gallons of fuel. The legal reserves for a VFR fight is only 4 gallons. The problem with most general aviation airplanes is the lack of precision in the fuel system. The gauges will indicate "empty" long before the tanks reach the reserve levels of 2 gallons a side.

Landing with a fuel level that low requires careful planning and knowledge of actual fuel flows acquired from flying that particular aircraft. Additionally, many airplanes will have maneuvering limitations imposed because of the low quantities in the fuel tanks. These are some of the reasons many pilots agree flying to so low a fuel capacity is unsafe.

Why?

Because there are still many variables that can eliminate a four-gallon reserve. These variables include weather, the ATC environment near the destination, a miss-rigged or faulty carburetor, or other engine problems causing higher than normal fuel flows. The list can go on and the consequences dire.

An example of a situation involving air traffic control could be something complex, or maybe as simple as the preceding plane in front of you having an incident on the only runway within 50 nm. For a 100-knot airplane, that will virtually eliminate the FAA mandated 30-minute reserve. You cannot plan for these types of events. You can plan for other, more normal, events. Take weather, for example.

If the weather is questionable, a pilot has options. The pilot can postpone the flight, the destination can be changed to some other airport nearby, or if the pilot is rated, he or she can choose to file IFR.

Now, here's the important thing about "leftovers."

When planning and flying instruments, wise pilots will know exactly how much fuel they will have after landing, regardless of landing at the destination or the alternate. More importantly, they will know exactly what their options are for the available fuel onboard.

Options? Yes, options.

Take for example, an IFR flight. The options available for the instrument pilot includes two: how many approaches can you shoot at the destination trying to get in and how long can you hold waiting for the weather to improve. This boils down to how many approaches can you make? How long can you hold? And most importantly, when do you execute?

Let's take a look at a typical instrument flight from Montgomery, AL to Orlando Executive, FL flown in a Piper Seminole along the preferred low-altitude airways. Let's assume a heavy-handed pilot who typically flies at high power settings resulting in a fuel flow of 20 gph. The flight, according to flight planning, will involve 2 hours, 24 minutes and 49 gallons of fuel. If everything goes as it should and the aircraft lands on the first approach, there will remain 53 gallons of fuel out of the 102 gallons useable.

If the weather is below minimums, however, the pilot must make some important decisions. In most cases, the pilot can try approach after approach in hopes of getting in, or he or she might elect to reduce power to max conserve and wait the weather out. The key is for the pilot to know how many approaches are possible, or how long to hold. Most important is counting those approaches carefully and not shooting one too many, or knowing exactly what time to depart the hold for the alternate.

If the alternate for this flight is Tampa International, the flight from Orlando Executive to KTPA requires 34 minutes and 12 gallons of fuel. Adding the fuel together for the leg from KMGM to KORL (49 gallons) with the fuel required from KORL to KTPA (12 gallons) and the reserve requirement of 15 gallons, the minimum fuel required for the flight is 76 gallons. This includes one approach at KORL and then immediately proceeding to the alternate of Tampa.

Subtracting 76 gallons from the initial useable fuel load of 102 gallons leaves the pilot with 26 gallons of excess fuel, or "leftovers." Now the question becomes one of what to do with the excess fuel.

If the weather at the destination looks as though it will allow a successful approach at some point, the pilot can make multiple approaches trying to get in. How many? Assuming a lower fuel flow of 18 gph and 15 minutes per approach, 26 gallons divided by 18 equals one hour and 26 minutes. Dividing 1.4 by .25 equals a total of five approaches (rounded down).

If this is the intent of the pilot, what he or she needs to do is mark each approach somewhere on the nav card. In other words, there needs to be a tick marked at each missed approach in order to shoot no more approaches than fuel will allow. I had a friend do that once—he lost track of the approaches and his fuel—he almost did not make it. In this example, after the fifth approach, the pilot needs to pick up the clearance to the alternate and go. When arriving in Tampa and shooting the approach and landing, the pilot will have exactly 15 gallons (45 minutes) fuel reserve at shutdown.

If the pilot should choose to hold, he or she needs to know a few more numbers. Assume the flight departs KMGM at 0400Z, and flight time is 2:24, arrival at KORL will be 0624Z. With a fuel surplus of 26 gallons and assuming an endurance powering setting with a fuel flow of 14 gph, the pilot has the option to hold for one hour and 51 minutes.

After entering the hold, the pilot needs to write down the "drop dead time" for departure to Tampa somewhere clearly visible on the nav card. The time to depart for Tampa should be noted both in GMT and local time if needed. Arrival at KORL 0624Z (0242L DST) plus 1:51 in holding means departure for Tampa must happen at 0815Z (0415L DST). After the 34-minute flight to Tampa, the fuel supply will be right at the 45-minute legal reserve.

The bottom line is this: pilots can never have too much fuel. The fuel they do have, they need to know how to use it.

Wisely...

Essays From Aviation History

Driving Around Tampa

I rarely sit in the backseat, but here I am with my wife looking out the back windows. Her dad is driving and her mom navigating as we transit around the city where we all grew up. For me, it barely resembles the place I remember. There are landmarks which will never change; the twist of the river, the bend of the shoreline. Then there are other landmarks I thought would always be the same and they changed overnight, such as the city's skyline. I recall coming home from my first semester in college and new high rise buildings were up in the downtown area.

We drive by the Alessi Bakery, a Tampa landmark in its own right. My father-in-law mentions they make the best Cuban sandwiches ever. "The secret is in the bread," he says. His daughter agrees. I think back on all the Cuban sandwiches I have eaten in my life. Only the great ones came from Tampa. And they were really good. During the time I was in college and later served in the Navy, I remember restaurants and delis calling a sandwich on their menu a "Cuban Sandwich." It was not. And I would always find myself thinking of Tampa.

Tampa is very rich in history. This was the place from which Teddy Roosevelt's Rough Riders began their Cuban campaign. In World War II, the older local population remembers Tampa International Airport as Drew Field and the other base, now MacDill AFB, trained B-26 pilots. In North Tampa where a beer brewery is now located, just south of the University of South Florida, lie the remnants of the runways of another long forgotten airfield.

The B-26 was tricky to fly and some inexperienced pilots based at MacDill weren't so skillful, or lucky, with the "Marauder." If you ever heard the phrase, "One a day, in Tampa Bay," it was the B-26 which gave us the saying. Too many young airmen died trying to master the bomber.

We travel through neighborhoods I remember from my youth. I think of the times I wished I lived in one of these neighborhoods rather than where we lived. Now, those neighborhoods aren't as nice as they were 40 years ago. In the years since, someone cut the trees, widened the roads, and inserted expressways into once beautiful and quiet neighborhoods. These actions, of course, crippled each locality and the once pristine homes in which owners took great pride now look like derelicts.

It is such a strange feeling, sitting in the backseat watching the scenes of Tampa drift by the window. I well remember parts of the city; then there are some things completely out of place. I find myself wishing I could go back in time, to the Tampa of the 1960s. I think of my Cuban grandparents, the days in school, and all my friends.

Then I realize something else — I really want a Cuban sandwich.

The Barnstormers

After the First World War, aviators returned to America in search of their fortunes in aviation. For a mere $400 or $500, they were able to acquire training aircraft from the government, the most common being the venerable Curtiss JN-4D "Jenny." During the period after the war, almost every school-aged child knew of the Jenny and hoped to fly one of the wood and fabric aircraft.

For a mere $3, the pilots, commonly known as gypsy pilots or barnstormers, flew the open cockpit airplanes carrying passengers aloft around their towns. Usually, it was a brave and hardy soul who flew with the early barnstormers. The barnstormers' Jennys were typically in ill repair with fabric patches covering damaged surfaces and engines that leaked oil and quit running with little or no warning. For those who dared fly with the gypsy pilots, it meant the possibility of personal harm due to airframe or engine failure, enduring hot rocker cover grease and oil sprayed in their face, and the loss of $3 which would go to put gasoline in the Jenny and food into the pilot.

So, what did a brave passenger get for the cost of $3?

They got the chance to fly above their home; to see green fields as never before; a chance to look over the horizon; to view cars that looked like toys and friends who were no larger than dolls; and if one were brave enough, they may possibly see the world from upside down while listening to the wind whistling in the wires.

During the 1920s and early 1930s, the barnstormers made their impression on America by introducing the country to aviation. Although the method of this introduction was sometimes less than optimal, the gypsy pilots left an indelible mark on the country. By 1925, almost everyone in America became aware of aviation in some manner or form.

The gypsy pilots and their Jennys lit a match to shine on the aviation industry. Unknown to them at the time, there was a wind starting to blow and that wind was fanning the fires.

As America moved from the second decade of that century into the third, airplanes and technology improved, in some cases, drastically. As a result, flying became a more accepted and safer means of travel toward the end of the 1920s.

Remember When

Remember back when traveling by the airlines was really special? Everyone dressed in their very best to "take a flight" somewhere. Passengers were well mannered, the food was good, airline employees were happy, and massive radial engines made by Pratt & Whitney powered the huge airliners. And TSA stood for something other than the Transportation Security Administration.

Back in those days my favorite airliner was the triple-tailed Lockheed Constellation. The "Connie," as many who flew as both crew and passengers referred to her, was truly a magnificent aircraft. Lockheed dates the initial design back to 1937. The company made the first flight of the aircraft on January 9, 1943.

Four P&W Wright R-3350 18-cylinder radial engines powered the Connie with a total of 13,000 horsepower. This gave the airliner a maximum speed of 377 mph, or 327 knots. At altitude, she could cruise at 295 knots with a maximum range of 5400 statute miles, or 4700 nautical miles. This airplane was no slouch and she was far ahead of her time.

From the first flight in 1943, the Connies flew in service until 1967. The military kept her on until 1978. Several organizations operated the airplane; she flew in the livery of Trans World Airlines (TWA), Eastern Airlines (EAL), Pan American World Airways (PA), the United States Navy and Air Force. Several foreign flagged airlines also operated the Connie, the most notable being Air France, KLM, Lufthansa, and Trans-Canada Airlines (the predecessor to Air Canada).

The normal complement of crew members on the flight deck included the pilot, the first officer, a flight engineer, navigator, and radio operator. The number of cabin attendants depended on the passenger load per flight.

Concerning loads, the passenger seat configuration usually ranged from 60 to 95; with higher density seating, the total passenger capacity exceeded 100. The empty weight of the aircraft was approximately 79,000 to 80,000 pounds with a maximum takeoff weight of 137,500 pounds.

When the Connie came off the line, she did so in spectacular fashion. This extremely powerful and gorgeously sleek airplane set numerous records on a routine basis. In April of 1944 the second production aircraft flew from Burbank, CA to Washington, DC in 6 hours and 57 minutes. The president of TWA, Jack Frye, and the legendary Howard Hughes flew the aircraft. On the flight back to California, the two stopped at Wright Field in Ohio. They had the privilege of flying Orville Wright on his last flight more than 40 years after his historic first flight on December 17, 1903.

For the Connie, jets came just a little too soon. When the Boeing 707 and the Douglas DC-8 began taking over the market share of airline travel in the early 1960s, many airline companies put the Connies out to pasture.

When they did, it was a shame.

There remains no more an elegant and beautiful airliner than the Connie.

The Connie

First Flight

If you are a pilot, or if you are not but have a serious interest in aviation history, you owe it to yourself to visit *First Flight* on the outer banks in North Carolina. This is the place where the Wright brothers conducted their flight experiments that culminated in mankind's first powered flight.

At the turn of the previous century, Kitty Hawk and Kill Devil Hill were, by the most gracious of descriptions, bleak and barren. The wind on the coast blew constant and steady, making the location ideal for the brothers' flight experiments.

The Wrights became interested in flight after their father, Bishop Wright gave them a toy helicopter. The idea of flight intrigued the boys for the first time at the ages of 7 and 11 at the time. Later in their lives, in the summer of 1896, Orville contracted typhoid fever. Wilbur took care of his sibling and the two continued their habit of reading.

Orville and Wilbur Wright

In August of that year in Germany, Otto Lilienthal crashed one of his many gliders. He sustained severe injuries which led to his death days after the accident on August 10. While Orville recovered from the typhoid fever, he and Wilbur read newspaper accounts of Lilienthal's death.

This, too, further fueled their fire to fly.

Both brothers, along with their other five siblings, grew up in an environment which well prepared them for their pursuit of flight. Orville would later write about the encouragement their parents provided their children in "intellectual interests" and other topics which "aroused curiosity."

Self-educated engineers, the Wrights investigated the problems of flight from a scientific approach. They perfected much of their research in areas that few had ever addressed. The remarkable thing about their work was that their theoretical mathematics in aerodynamics hit right on the mark.

In the years leading up to the first flight, the brothers did a great deal of observation, research, and experimenting. They watched birds fly, developed and flew different kites, analyzed engines, and built their own for the flight. They also produced the first practical "air screw," or as we know it today, the propeller.

All of the brothers' research and work paid off in 1903 on December 17, when they flew the Wright Flyer four times that historic day.

Orville Wright won the distinction of becoming the first pilot in the history of the world. His flight lasted a mere 12 seconds while flying just under 7 mph. The distance of 120 feet is less than the wingspan of many of today's modern aircraft.

It was this first lift-off from the starting rails that Coast Guardsman John T. Daniels recorded by firing the shutter on the camera Orville Wright pre-positioned before the flight. In addition to Daniels, four others were eyewitnesses to history. On the day of the first flights, the brothers would fly 120 feet, then 175 feet and 200 feet respectively. The last flight, flown by Wilbur, would take the airplane 852 feet over 59 seconds before weather damaged the aircraft after the last flight.

What the brothers accomplished on that December day is by definition, the greatest achievement in the history of the world. Had they failed, Neil Armstrong would not have walked on the moon 65 years, seven months later.

The incredible thing about the brothers' first flights is not only did they invent the airplane, they taught themselves how to fly.

The Sunshine Skyway

Yesterday my wife, her parents, and I visited her sister in Bradenton. It was a nice afternoon — except for the Gator's game — that was a pretty hard loss to the Seminoles. Afterward, we started home to my in-law's place in Tampa.

The trip required crossing the Sunshine Skyway Bridge. Each time I cross the Skyway, especially at night, I find my mind wandering all over the place.

This city is rich in history and culture. Stories of Fort Brooke and the early days come to mind. I think of the Rough Riders and Teddy Roosevelt massing near the shipyards preparing for their voyage to Cuba during the Spanish American War.

When looking out on the dark waters of Tampa Bay, the birth of scheduled airline flying comes to mind. It was here Tony Jannus piloted the very first scheduled commercial airline flight between St. Petersburg and Tampa, flying in a bi-wing seaplane for the St. Petersburg Tampa Airboat Line. The inaugural flight took place on January 1, 1914.

In World War II, MacDill Field played an important role in training Army Air Corps pilots for the war effort. MacDill was an advanced training base for the B-26 Marauder, which was one of the most advanced and difficult airplanes to fly at the time. Several Marauders crashed on land and 13 ditched into Tampa Bay during a 14 month period shortly after the war began. This created the local saying, "One a day, in Tampa Bay" among the civilian populace and military pilots alike.

Many pilots believed the Marauder was incapable of flying on one engine. The true problem with the airplane was that it had powerful engines coupled with a small wing area, vertical fin, and rudder surfaces. It required precise handling to fly the airplane on one engine. After Jimmy Doolittle and other experienced aviators proved the airplane capable and briefed the inexperienced pilots on proper procedures, B-26s stopped dropping into the bay.

From the top of the bridge, I can see where Tampa International Airport brightens the night sky. It was at KTPA I cut my teeth as an instrument pilot (see Cutting Teeth, page 105). I think back to all the times I landed on 36L with fog so thick I almost didn't make it in. But I always did. Never once did I have to call up the company to tell them I had to divert somewhere else. I am glad those days flying Part 135 are behind me.

As we start down from the top of the span, I think about the bridge itself. The original bridge linked St. Petersburg and the Bradenton area in 1954. Later, state engineers added another span to the first.

Those two spans served the state well, but with a mix of tragedy. By media and official estimates, some 130 people chose to jump from the bridge to end their lives.

Additionally, the Coast Guard lost 23 men when its ship, the USCGC Blackthorne collided head on with a cruise ship, the Capricorn. This accident happened on January 28, 1980.

A very short time later on May 5, 1980, I remember waking to the excited voice of Captain Al Ford, the Tampa area traffic announcer for WDAE 1250 AM radio. At 7:33 on a very stormy morning, a freighter, the Summit Venture, collided with the bridge while trying to navigate under the bridge in hard rain. In the fashion of the worst Hollywood disaster movies, the western span of the bridge collapsed. In the poor visibility of the driving rain, a Greyhound bus and six cars plunged 150 feet into the bay. Between the bus and the cars, 35 people perished.

After the state completed its investigations, it designed and built a completely new bridge just east of where the old bridge once stood. Workers tore down the old structure, but state officials were wise enough to leave the old roadways in place. They now serve as fishing piers. Each year since, I have been meaning to catch some snook off the fishing piers.

Maybe this year.

A Brand New Airplane

If asked, many do not know the significance of the Ryan NYP, much less able to describe the airplane from that name. The NYP is one of the most important airplanes ever designed, built, and flown and today, resides in the Smithsonian National Air & Space Museum in Washington, DC.

While few know the airplane as the Ryan NYP, almost everyone knows the aircraft by its given name, *The Spirit of St. Louis*. The airplane, registered as N-X-211, is truly one of the most important airplanes ever to fly.

Charles Linbergh

The story of this amazing aircraft begins when Charles Lindbergh proposed his flight to businessmen in St. Louis. Once approved and financing arranged, the young aviator was off to San Diego to work with members of the Ryan Airlines Company. They would design and build the airplane that would take Lindbergh across the Atlantic and into history.

The Ryan Airlines Company based the design of the airplane on Donald Hall's previous mail plane, the Ryan M-2. This saved time and money in creating the airplane, which successfully won the $25,000 Orteig Prize for the first crossing of the Atlantic Ocean.

The main difference between the M-2 and the NYP was the size of the wing. The Ryan engineers increased the wingspan of the M-2 10 feet in order to create the wing surface area required to lift the aircraft and 2700 pounds of fuel. Combined with the empty weight of the aircraft, gross takeoff weight for the airplane totaled 5135 pounds.

Lindbergh, Hall, and others at the Ryan Company worked together tirelessly on the airplane. From the time they made the changes to the design of the M-2, until the first flight of the NYP, the process took only 60 days. By the way, the "NYP" designation was short for "New York to Paris."

The airplane was a marvel of the time. Many considered the NYP as one of the most advanced designs of the 1920s. The airplane carried 450 gallons of aviation fuel in five separate fuel tanks, requiring Lindbergh to be on his guard while keeping track of which tank was selected and how much fuel remained in each throughout the flight. The range of the airplane was 4100 miles at a cruising speed of approximately 105 mph. This resulted in an endurance of 39 hours.

The Spirit of St. Louis had one of the most sophisticated engines of the time, the Wright J-5C "Whirlwind." It produced 223 hp and many in aviation considered the engine a mechanical marvel. Originally, the engineers designed the motor to run for 9000 hours.

The first flight of the NYP, flown at Dutch Flats at San Diego lasted only 20 minutes. Lindbergh flew a second flight of five minutes. Over the next ten days, they would fly the airplane 23 times for a total flight time of four hours and 15 minutes.

On May 10, Lindbergh departed San Diego for New York, with a stop at Lambert Field in St. Louis. On May 12, Lindbergh landed in

New York and following a few test flights, readied the airplane for the flight to Paris. When they departed for Paris, the airplane, still considered brand new, had flown 32 times and only had 27 hours and 25 minutes logged.

Takeoff from Roosevelt Field occurred at 7:52 a.m. on May 20, 1927. After flying for 33.5 hours, Lindbergh landed at Le Bourget in Paris at 10:22 local time on the 21st.

Lindbergh would fly the airplane over the coming year before turning the historic aircraft over the Smithsonian in Washington one year and one day after the first flight. *The Spirit of St. Louis* had flown of 174 times for total flight time 489 hours and 28 minutes.

As she hangs in the Smithsonian's Air & Space Museum today, she can still be regarded as a brand new airplane, or maybe an almost new plane.

Jimmy Stewart

Jimmy Stewart, born James Maitland Stewart in Indiana, Pennsylvania on May 20, 1908, was one of the most beloved movie actors of the Twentieth Century. Stewart was a gentle soul who also happened to be an excellent piano player. Moreover and unknown to many, he was a combat pilot and military leader of extraordinary aptitude.

Like many early in the first century of flight, Stewart had a natural interest in aviation. He fostered his desire to fly like others — by building model airplanes in the basement of his parents' home. His interest in flying, mathematics, and science took him to Princeton University where he excelled in architecture. He blended his love of aviation and architecture into his studies; he did so well, he acquired a scholarship to graduate school for further study in the field.

While at Princeton, he began acting. As with his studies, he enjoyed acting and excelled in his efforts. Before long, he was a full blown, bona fide movie star in Hollywood. He also stayed true to his desire to fly, acquiring his private pilot certificate in 1935.

Three years later, he passed his commercial pilot checkride. Many considered Stewart a proficient and serious pilot.

In 1940, the military actually drafted Stewart into service, but he failed the height and weight requirements. He was too light. However, his background and family history obliged him to continue competing for a place in the service. Stewart's ancestors on both sides fought in the War Between the States and on his father's side, his family fought in the Revolutionary War. Stewart was more than compelled to serve, to do his part.

In March 1941, he tried again, this time meeting the weight requirements. He became Private James Stewart, movie star-soldier. He was the first of many movie stars to join the military during World War II.

Jimmy Stewart, bomber pilot

Competing for a flight slot, Stewart finally found himself in flight school. After graduation, he worried the Army would keep him stateside performing instructor duties. Through his single-minded perseverance, he finally won a position in a B-24 combat squadron.

August 1943 found him flying across the Atlantic as a member of the 703rd Bombardment Squadron. He later took command of the 453rd based at Old Buckenham Airfield in England, commonly referred to as "Old Buc." It was as the commander of the 453rd that Stewart truly shined.

He was a natural born leader. Among his men, he was not Jimmy Stewart, the actor; he was Major James Stewart, and later Lieutenant Colonel James Stewart, United States Army Air Corps.

Stewart was not one of those commanding officers who told his men to go fly the hard missions. When it was time to fly a difficult run, Stewart was out in front, in the lead ship. He was a tireless worker. He knew there was a job to be finished and he was one to work with his men, rather than giving orders for mission accomplishment.

Jimmy Stewart did not work all the time, however, and was capable of pulling off some really impressive practical jokes. As the group operations officer, Stewart and his assistant, Captain Andy Low, needed to get away from the daily grind of their duties. They needed some flight time and decided to get it by going over to Stewart's previous base and buzzing his former commanding officer. They got themselves into a little hot water with that one but, in the middle of war, they were able to get away with it. After the chewing out, they probably became better leaders. Each went on to become general officers.

One of my favorite photographs of Jimmy Stewart was shot right after the war. He and his men were returning from England on board the *Queen Elizabeth* huddled together. Stewart's men looked tired. They looked as though they had just won a war. There was Stewart in the middle of them, Colonel Stewart. Not Jimmy Stewart the movie star, it was bomber pilot Stewart, leader and protector of his men.

Like the others, he was tired. And he looked thankful the war was over.

The Juan T. Trippe

These days, if you don't know who Juan T. Trippe is, the old airplane guys can almost excuse you because we have now moved so far down the timeline away from the glorious days of airline travel. This was a time when Pan American World Airways ruled the skies. For those who don't know of Mr. Trippe, he is the man who created the airline.

Juan Trippe was born just before the turn of the century. While a student at Yale, the United States entered World War I. Trippe took a leave of absence to pursue flight training and a commission in the United States Navy. The war ended before he had an opportunity to fly combat, so when released from active duty, he returned to Yale to graduate in 1921.

After becoming bored with Wall Street, Trippe created the Long Island Airways which served as an air-taxi operation for New York's rich. He then worked with an airline known as Colonial Air Transport, a company running airmail in the mid 1920s. Afterward, he became interested in starting service in the Caribbean, so he created the Aviation Company of the Americas. This is the company, headquartered in Florida, which would later become Pan American Airways.

Trippe, along with Howard Hughes, Eddie Rickenbacker, and others who many considered the leaders in the new airline industry, made air travel what it is today. Pan American Airways began business with service between Key West, FL and Havana, Cuba. From there, expansion became rapid.

Trippe was instrumental in expanding Pan American into the Pacific Ocean where the company flew their trademark Clipper flying boats. Additionally, Trippe became responsible for many of the innovations used in the airline industry of the time.

In the early 1960s, Pan American led the way into the jet age by ordering Boeing 707s. Through his friendship with Boeing's Bill Allen, Trippe was almost single-handedly responsible for the creation of the Boeing 747. In the latter part of the decade and into the 1970s, travelers the world over recognized the 747 as the symbol for international jet travel, often associating the plane with Pan American Airways.

Trippe won *The Tony Jannus Award* in 1965 for his extraordinary work and contributions to the airline industry. He maintained the helm of Pan American World Airways until 1968.

The first Boeing 747 ever built never served as an airliner; it served as a test bed for much of the evaluation the engineers wanted to complete on the new airframe. Pan American World Airways purchased the second Boeing 747 off the assembly line. The company named the airplane *The Juan T. Trippe* in honor of the man who started it all. This airplane was the very first 747 to carry passengers. This particular 747 should have won a well-deserved place in aviation history. Today, *The Juan T. Trippe* should be the main display in a premier aviation museum. Sadly, she is not.

Unfortunately, as with many old airliners, *The Juan T. Trippe* went to the desert to sit outside in dry storage in Mojave, CA. From there, buyers purchased the airplane for $1,000,000 and had it disassembled. For another $100,000, they had the pieces and parts of the airplane shipped to South Korea where they converted it into a restaurant.

The couple who bought the airplane did have a sense of aviation history, which led to the original purchase. This unusual aviation slant was to be the draw for their restaurant. Unfortunately, their plan did not work. The restaurant failed and the airplane sat abandoned. Knowing the aircraft's significance in history, the couple worked diligently to find a buyer for the historic craft. This, too, ended in failure.

In 2010, *The Juan T. Trippe* met her final end. She was shredded and sent to the scrap yard.

First Flight

107 Years

Published December 17, 2010

A century plus seven years. It is almost too much to comprehend, especially when you give thought to the amazing accomplishments we have made since.

It was 107 years ago today the Wright Brothers officially "cracked the code" on getting heavier than air devices into the sky. Many today have little knowledge of the significance of the event; for them, the convenience of crossing the nation or an ocean in a few hours time is the most important aspect of flying.

Somehow, history has passed by those who know little about aviation. They have overlooked the impact flying has had on their lives, taking our modern miracles completely for granted. At the start of the last century, the field of aviation was almost non-existent. Very few possessed the vision to drive events beyond that first flight of 107 years ago.

As history records, however, a few industrious individuals became enamored with the idea of perfecting flight. At first, progress was slow, but as technology, materials, and research advanced, so also did the new commerce that would soon become the aviation industry.

Sopwith Camel

Over the years, the greatest technological advances occurred during times of war and the aviation industry was no exception. When World War I erupted in Europe, the airplanes of the times were barely able to get out of their own way, much less fight against others. At the start of the war, aerial combatants would literally fly alongside taking pot shots at each other with their side arms. By war's end, the early aviators perfected aerial combat maneuvering and aircraft design advanced very rapidly.

Between wars, it was the time of the barnstormers, the refinement of airmail, and the development of radios and instruments allowing pilots to fly in poor weather. Charles Lindbergh would fly the Atlantic on May 21, 1927 and a little over two years later, Jimmy Doolittle became the first pilot to takeoff, fly a course, and land an airplane completely blind — strictly on instruments.

Regarding airline aviation, the 1930s was an incredible time. A mere 32 years after the Wright's first flight, the Douglas DC-3 made her maiden voyage. Many of those early DC-3s fly still today, a testament to the ruggedness of the airframe and the foresight of the engineers who designed her.

Maritime aviation allowed for the start of World War II on December 7, 1941 when the Japanese employed six aircraft carriers to deploy 360 attack aircraft with another 48 scout and combat air patrol aircraft to attack Pearl Harbor. While the Japanese only bloodied our noses, the fight was still in us and the United States returned the favor on April 18, 1942. Flying from the single aircraft carrier, the *USS Hornet*, 16 B-25 Mitchell bombers crewed by 79 volunteers and led by Lt. Col. James H. Doolittle, attacked the heart of Japan.

As the war escalated, so too, did the technology allowing ever greater advancement in aviation. At the start of the war, some of the aircraft in the US inventory actually included open cockpit biplanes; by the end of the war, we were flying pressurized B-29 *Superfortresses* and our fighters were capable of almost 500 mph. Then, the sound barrier fell to Chuck Yeager and the Air Force on October 14, 1947.

Douglas DC-3

At the start of the 1950s, the Korean War erupted and so did the age of the jet fighter. Both the Russians and Chinese, as well as the United States, refined the use of jet fighters during this period. When we moved beyond the hostilities of the Korean conflict and into the mid '50s and the competition for space raged, the technological race remained as alive and well as in the first half of the 20th Century.

As we stretched beyond the atmosphere, we began designing vehicles with the potential to carry us to the moon. While the space race continued, the airline industry began to see

Boeing 707

expansion also. With the use of turbojets and the creation of the
Boeing 707, aerial transportation moved from the lower altitudes to
higher "flight levels."

After John F. Kennedy was elected president in 1960, he made
the proclamation the United States would go to the moon, "...by
the end of this decade." And we did.

Apollo 11
lifting from
Cape Kennedy
on
July 16, 1969

Then we went further than the moon, although not with people, faster around the world, higher into the fringes of the atmosphere, and built airplanes of which no one before the 20th Century could have ever comprehended.

One hundred and seven years ago, the common man's transportation depended on horses, mules, and buggies. At the time the Wrights flew, no one other than Jules Verne and H.G. Wells ever imagined we, the human race, could and would, walk on the moon.

As we go to bed this evening of the 107th anniversary of the first flight, one wonders what humanity might attain over the next 107 years.

Heroes

My student and I finished our flight a little early and when we returned to the ramp, I saw an early model Cessna 210 sitting in front of the flight dispatch building. From afar, the airplane looked good. As I approached it, it looked even better.

The interior was in good shape. I could see no corrosion on the airframe, and the avionics were up to date. As I was admiring the airplane, an older gentleman approached.

He was obviously the pilot of the 210. "Want to take a closer look?" he asked as he opened the pilot's door.

"Yes, I would, if it would be okay," I replied.

"Sure," he said as he placed his briefcase on the right seat. Then we began talking about old Cessnas. It was obvious he was a pilot's pilot and had been around Cessnas quite a while. We talked of the merits of the 210 and other Cessnas. Finally, I said I had to go meet my next student and he said he had to get on with his flight.

I enjoyed my short little discussion with the 210 pilot. As he climbed into the airplane, I walked into dispatch and met my friend, Rich.

"Do you know who you're just talking to?" Rich asked.

"I don't know — some old 210 pilot who really knew a lot about the airplane."

"Oh, I am sure he knows about 210 as well as many other airplanes."

"What do you mean?" I asked.

Scott Crossfield

"That was Scott Crossfield."

I jerked my head around to see the 210 taxiing away from the ramp. *Wow, a true American hero*, I thought.

While I was talking to him, he came across as simply another Cessna pilot. During our discussion, I had the fleeting thought I would enjoy sitting down and picking this man's brain a little more deeply, to gain more of his knowledge of Cessnas. I knew he would be one of those pilots who would fit in nicely with our little group of Cessna pilots at the home field.

And then, he turns out to be Scott Crossfield! *The* Scott Crossfield. Today, I wonder how many young people learning how to fly even know the name Scott Crossfield. I question how many know of his history and his contributions to the field of aviation.

Crossfield was born October 2, 1921 and grew up in California and Washington. He enlisted in the Navy and fought in World War II as a Navy fighter pilot. After the war, he acquired both his baccalaureate and master's degrees in aeronautical engineering. Then he began his work as a test pilot at Edwards Air Force Base in California.

On November 28, 1953 while working for the National Advisory Committee for Aeronautics' (NACA), Crossfield became the fastest human alive when he piloted the Douglas D-558-II Skyrocket at twice the speed of sound. Later, after joining North American Aviation, Crossfield became instrumental in the design of the X-15.

Crossfield went on to become a division vice president for Eastern Airlines, then a senior vice president at Hawker Siddeley, and finally, he served the U.S. House of Representatives on their Committee for Science and Technology.

On that day in the late 1990s when I met him on the ramp, I think Crossfield was content with being merely Scott, just another Cessna pilot.

Mankind's Greatest Navigational Achievement

Traveling from one place on the earth to another can be a phenomenal accomplishment. To get from one position on the globe precisely to a predetermined destination somewhere else is, in a word, amazing. How were we able to get from here to there? What do you consider the most significant act of navigation?

If given a little thought, the voyage of Christopher Columbus turns into an astonishing story. On August 3, 1492, Columbus left the Spanish town of Palos de la Frontera on his three ships, the *Santa Maria*, the *Pinta*, and the *Niña*. Only 90 men made that first voyage; 40 on board the *Santa Maria*, 26 on the *Pinta*, and only 24 on the *Niña*. They were bound for their first stop on the voyage to the New World, the Canary Islands.

Of the men on board, Christopher Columbus was the "learned navigator." In his heart and mind, he knew the world was round. For the most part, however, the crew did not believe the world was round and by the time they were at sea for five weeks without sight of land, there was talk of mutiny.

As the rumblings of insubordination gained momentum, at about two o'clock in the morning on October 12, 1492, a sailor aboard the *Pinta*, Rodrigo de Triana, sighted land and sounded the alarm. Later that day Columbus and his men set foot for the first time in the New World.

While Columbus' voyage was a fascinating navigational achievement, think about this: the Polynesians canoed across thousands of miles of ocean to find and settle the Hawaiian Islands. This they did about 200 years after the death of Christ.

They accomplished their trans-Pacific crossings without modern navigational instruments. There were no sextants, no compasses—nothing. To determine angles, they used their hands, held perpendicular to the deck of the canoe at arm's length. They also recited songs, passed down through the generations from one family navigator to the next.

The voyage was a challenge, both physically and mentally for everyone, but in particular, for the navigators. They did their job not only without instruments, but also without charts. They did so by memorizing the stars at night, the wind, the currents, and by using the sun during the day.

From these rudimentary basics, the Polynesians not only canoed to Hawaii from the Marquesas Islands, they returned and sailed again—again, across thousands of miles of open ocean. This was an incredible feat of navigation. However, was it the most incredible navigational achievement ever?

Personally, I believe the most fantastic navigational miracle of all time was the return of the Apollo 13 astronauts, who launched on April 11, 1970. After their craft suffered crippling explosions and loss of the electrical system, there was a very high probability they were not going to make it back.

Ever.

They lost critical mission equipment during the event, including the onboard computers required to "fly" the craft. Without the computers, the crew, consisting of James A. Lovell, John "Jack" Swigert, and Fred W. Haise, faced the challenge of "hand-flying" the vehicle back to earth.

The three of them, working as a team and in concert with ground personnel in Houston, lined up the Apollo spacecraft with their naked eyes. They also calculated how much of a burn was required to put their craft on the proper angle, and then they did it, completely by hand.

And everyone involved in the miraculous recovery did most of their mathematical calculations using *slide rules*.

Carrots and Night Flying

When I talk with my commercial pilot classes about radar, one of my favorite "extra point" test questions deals with carrots. None know the story of British ace, John Cunningham.

Cunningham was a Royal Air Force officer who went from boyhood to manhood almost overnight at the age of 23. On the front side of 23, many described Cunningham as being as close to an angel as possible without offending him. On the backside of 23, he was perhaps the most dangerous night-fighter pilot of the RAF.

What made Cunningham dangerous was his ability to "see" in the dark. Flying as a night fighter pilot, by war's end he totaled 20 kills. Of course, Cunningham's night vision was not the result of eating carrots, as the British High Command would have the world believe.

No, Cunningham's prowess as a fighter pilot was the result of the invention of radar.

Radar turned out to be a wonderful technology for the aviation industry over the last 60 years. By emitting radar waves and receiving the reflections of those waves as they bounced off hard targets, pilots are able to "radar map" the terrain, "see" rain, and in the case of fighter pilots, find enemy aircraft, regardless of the weather or time of day.

The ruse about carrots was the invention of the British military. In their quest to keep knowledge of radar from the Germans, each aircrew member with any knowledge of radar received the same briefing regarding what they should say if shot down and captured.

The universal story every British aviator would tell was that the British put the night-fighter pilots on a very high and strict diet of carrots for the beta-carotene. This improved their night vision allowing them to see German aircraft in the dark.

The Germans bought the story for a while, but only for a short while. The Germans quickly realized in order to improve a person's eyesight to the degree necessary for that kind of night vision, they would have to eat massive quantities of carrots at every meal. Additionally, they would have to have large snacks of carrots between each meal.

The interesting thing about the British High Command's story was that while the Germans failed to believe it for any length of time, the mothers and fathers of many children bought it hook, line, and sinker. To this day, parents still tell their children to eat their carrots so they can see at night.

After all, their parents told them the same thing, and their parents would never lie to them, would they?

Brothers to the Rescue, Hermanos Al Rescate

Geographically, Cuba is a wonderful place, truly a paradise. But, politically, it remains a mess.

Some of the recent news about Cuban politics includes the government finally admitting socialism does not work and the Cuban economic situation is broken. The Castro brothers are eagerly seeking relations with the United States over the last few years. The Cuban government continues to harass citizens who dare to speak publicly about governmental failings. There are other, graver, indicators things are not quite right in Paradise. If life were good in Cuba, citizens from all over the world would try to immigrate to the island. As it is, every day, Cubans risk their lives trying to escape to America and other, free destinations.

A mere 90 miles separates the two nations. Many Cubans look to the north and know it is only a short boat trip or a long raft ride to freedom. Many get into trouble on the rafts in the Florida Straits. Who is there to look out for them? Who will give them humanitarian aid?

It used to be The Brothers to the Rescue, El Hermanos Rescate.

Volunteer pilots and observers flew the Florida Straits looking for rafters. Their mission was humanitarian. They were devoted to helping rafters survive who were in trouble at sea. The pilots and their crews dropped flotation gear and drinking water to rafting Cubans in need. They were there to help.

Who were these volunteer pilots and observers?

They were free Cubans; they were the sons and daughters of Cuban refugees born in the United States. They were human beings genuinely concerned for the safety and well-being of their fellow man.

They are young people like Carlos Costa.

Carlos Costa was born in the United States of Cuban heritage. As with many, he dreamed of flying and found himself attending college to learn to fly. After graduation, Carlos began working in South Florida in airport management. While working, he continued to accrue flight time. He dreamed of flying professionally which meant he had to build his flight experience. One way he did this was through volunteer flying with *El Hermanos Rescate*.

Costa was one of the more stalwart volunteer pilots. He was aggressive at flying his missions, always ready to fly. He was good, as I remember. I had the opportunity to fly with him as a check pilot on his commercial checkride. Carlos possessed a quiet confidence I knew would serve him well in his flying career.

Unfortunately, the Cuban government cut his flying career short.

On February 24, 1996 while searching for Cuban rafters who might be in trouble, Carlos was piloting one Cessna 337 Skymaster on a rescue mission with two others. A Cuban MIG-29 shot down two of the three Skymasters. Carlos Alberto Costa was one of four victims lost at sea that afternoon.

When word of the shootdown reached the school and that one of the pilots was one of our graduates, we were all saddened. When I learned Carlos was one of the victims, I felt a particular loss; he was a bright young man, a talented pilot, and had a wonderful future.

Rest easy, young airman.

The World's First Supersonic Ejection

In 1955, George Smith was 31-years-old, unmarried, stood 6'1" and weighed 220 pounds. It was a Saturday morning. He was off work and on his way to the grocery store, but stopped by his office to drop off some flight test reports on an acceptance flight he performed earlier in the week. North American Aviation dispatcher Bob Gallahue saw George walking to his car in the parking lot. He called out to George and asked if he would perform an acceptance flight for an F-100A in need of delivery to the Air Force.

Smith agreed to the flight.

He pulled on his flightsuit over his jeans, grabbed his helmet and headed to the flight line. Soon after, Smith found himself sitting in the *Super Sabre* at Los Angeles International, where North American Aviation, Inc. was located.

During the preflight checks, Smith noticed the stick forces fore and aft for pitch control seemed a little stiff or sluggish. He made note of it and did not believe the problem to be serious. Moments later, during this takeoff roll at rotation, Smith became more concerned with the nose heaviness of the aircraft.

He continued on to altitude busting through a layer at 8000 feet rocketing into the sky over the Pacific. At FL 350, he and the Super Sabre approached Mach 1. At 37,000 feet, the jet suddenly pitched over and started racing to the sea faster than the speed of sound.

Smith knew the odds were very poor for surviving a supersonic ejection. He also knew he had no possible hope of surviving the crash. With the engine idled and the speed brakes deployed, Smith tried to regain control of the stricken fighter. Passing 8000 feet on the way down, Smith realized he had run out of options.

He blew the canopy off; the sudden explosion and wind noise frightened him and he reflexively leaned forward, away from the noise. His seat position was bad for ejection at any speed, much less supersonic.

Smith remembers nothing beyond this point. Mathematical calculations performed during the investigation estimated the speed of the aircraft at Mach 1.05, 675 knots, or 777 miles per hour. When Smith exited the airplane, the rate of descent was 1140 feet per second. The engineers determined the ejection subjected Smith to 8000 pounds of aerodynamic force and a deceleration of 40g. On ejection, Smith lost his shoes and socks, his wristwatch, ring, his flight gloves, and helmet. After automatic seat-man separation, several panels of his parachute blew out with the high-speed deployment.

Following the ejection, Smith actually had a bit of luck. He fell into the Pacific Ocean less than 100 yards away from a fishing boat commanded by former Navy Rescue Specialist Art Berkell. Berkell reached Smith's location in less than 50 seconds and retrieved him from the water. The pilot was delirious and in shock; when asked about the airplane, Smith asked, "What airplane?"

Later, Smith would slip into unconsciousness and stay that way for five days. He remained hospitalized for months. Smith's body suffered so much damage that at first, doctors feared he would never recover, or see again. His internal organs were severely injured, his small intestines perforated, and his liver badly damaged. He would however, eventually recover and return to fly supersonic jets.

Because of Smith's ejection, aeromedical doctors gained great insight regarding the subject of high-speed ejections.

Eastern Flight 1320

Sixty-eight passengers and a crew of five prepared for takeoff in the evening of St. Patrick's Day, 1970. The flight, Eastern Airlines Newark to Boston Shuttle, Flight 1320, departed a little before 8:00 p.m. In the cockpit, the captain of the flight was 35-year-old Robert Wilbur Jr., a former Air Force pilot. His first officer, James Hartley, was 31.

During the early 1970s, it was common for passengers on the shuttle flights to pay for passage after take off, somewhat the same as paying bus fare. One passenger, John J. Divivo, told the flight attendant he did not have money for the fare and requested to see the captain.

He made this request with a .38 caliber revolver.

Wilbur, a brand new captain of only six months, was about to deal with a very real hijacking situation. When Divivo came into the cockpit, Wilbur and Hartley assumed the deranged man would request to go to Havana, Cuba—the normal destination for hijackings in those days. Divivo had a different, more sinister demand.

Divivo told the pilots to fly east, out to sea until they ran out of gas.

The pilots ignored him. Seconds later, the deranged gunman shot the first officer with no warning. Hartley collapsed and then Divivo turned the gun on the captain, shooting Wilbur in the arm. Moments later, Hartley regained consciousness and was up and out of his seat engaging the hijacker. He was able to wrest the weapon away from Divivo, shooting the hijacker three times, who then lost consciousness.

Mortally wounded, Hartley relapsed into unconsciousness. Wilbur declared an emergency, advising ATC that the hijacker had wounded his first officer and needed medical attention. He never mentioned the hijacker had also shot him. A few minutes later, when Divivo regained his senses, he started to rise from where he had fallen on the console between the two pilots. Wilbur, now in possession of the weapon, used it to beat the hijacker into unconsciousness again.

Wilbur did an outstanding job of flying the jet, getting it to the runway, landing, and dealing with ATC—all the while wounded. On landing, the authorities took Divivo into custody.

Divivo would never stand trial for his crimes; six months later while in prison, the hijacker managed to commit suicide by hanging himself in his jail cell.

Today, years after the event, Wilbur has reported to various news sources that he rarely thinks about the hijacking. Each time he does reflect on what happened, he always pays homage to James Hartley, the man he considers the true hero of the Flight 1320.

Able Dogs and Spads

March 18, 1945, the XBT2D-1 flew for the first time. It was another of the great designs by Ed Heinemann, the designer of a number of aircraft produced by the Douglas Aircraft Company. As with many of the aircraft Heinemann created, the Douglas XBT2D-1 was one that would serve the nation well for a long time.

Douglas created this airplane as a replacement for other carrier-borne aircraft such as the Helldiver and TBM Avenger. In the end, the airplane served its mission impressively for both the Navy and the Air Force. Although designed in the mid 1940s, the single-engine bomber served the military through both the Korean and Vietnam wars.

Powered by a Wright R-3350 of 2700 horsepower, the airplane was a lifting animal. She had an empty weight of just under 12,000 pounds, could carry a weapons load of 8000 pounds, and then enough gas to bring the gross weight up to 25,000 pounds in internal fuel tanks and 300-gallon drop tanks underneath each wing, as well as a 2000 gallon shaped tank on the centerline station.

This allowed the ADs stay airborne for an extraordinarily long time. Typically about 11 to 14 hours at a time.

Many a Navy pilot would launch from the deck of a carrier on a very long, low-mission or "sand blower" route. They would be the first airplane launched on a strike to head off at fuel flows of "max conserve" just above the waves. Just before going "feet dry" over hostile territory the pilots pushed up their throttles for more speed. Then they struck their targets, egressed as fast as their R-3350s could carry them back to the beach, and once feet wet again, the pilots throttled back to max conserve. The Spad pilots would find their way back to the carrier, landing after another four or five hours of flying to return to the boat. Often they were the last airplane trapped from the strike, on which they were the first launched.

The Spad pilots were a different lot. They were the cream of the crop when it came to providing air support for the ground troops and the rescue helicopters heading in to retrieve downed aviators. They were pilots the likes of men like Bernie Fisher, a major at the time, who won the Congressional Medal of Honor for landing his USAF A-1E on a battled damaged field to rescue another pilot who was shot down earlier.

A-1H VA-152 USS Oriskany 1966

Douglas produced almost 3200 of the aircraft for the military. The airplane was a part of the inventory from the mid-1940s into the 1970s. The pilots and maintainers who worked on the airplane either loved her or hated her, but she was always solid and dependable as a rock.

One thing was certain—the soldiers and marines who called the airplane in for close air support could always depend on the Spads and their pilots.

The *USS Langley*, CV-1

March 20, 1922 was an important day in the records of Naval Aviation. On this day, the United States Navy launched its first aircraft carrier.

The *USS Langley*, also known as CV-1, first sailed as a collier in the Navy. Naval engineers essentially placed a roof over the bulk supply ship to create a "flight deck" over the original structures of the *USS Jupiter*, AC-3.

Initially, the Mare Island Naval Shipyard in California laid down *Jupiter's* keel in October 1911. The shipyard first launched the ship on August 14, 1912. Commander Joseph Reeves served as her first commanding officer. She went on to serve in the Pacific and Atlantic Oceans, as well as the Gulf of Mexico.

Later, Navy officials ordered the ship to Navy Yard Norfolk for conversion into the Navy's first aircraft carrier. The purpose of the conversion was to "experiment" with the new idea of "seaborne aviation." On April 11, 1920, the Navy officially changed the ship's name to the *USS Langley* in honor of one of America's early pioneers of aviation, Samuel P. Langley. She was newly commissioned again on this date as the *USS Langley*, CV-1. Her new commanding officer, the first commanding officer of an aircraft carrier, was Commander Kenneth Whiting.

The first aircraft launched from the deck of the *Langley* was a Vought VE-7 piloted by Lt. Virgil Griffin on October 17, 1922.

Griffin was not the first pilot to take off from a ship; that honor belongs to Eugene Ely after he took off from the converted foredeck of the *USS Birmingham* on November 14, 1911.

The *Birmingham* was not an aircraft carrier, rather, she was a light cruiser. The *Langley*, on the other hand, was the Navy's first aircraft carrier. Even though 11 years had passed between the events of the first shipboard take off to the first take off from an aircraft carrier, the Navy could now lay claim to Naval Aviation. This was an important event.

With the launching of the *USS Langley*, the Navy truly entered the era of Naval Aviation. However, many still considered the concept of flying airplanes from the decks of aircraft carriers as only "an experiment." The process of developing practical application of air power at sea would face decades of trials and tribulations at the cost of much in terms of lives, aircraft, and injury.

No matter how difficult, no matter how dangerous, Navy pilots flying converted land-based aircraft pursued the idea of seaborne aerial warfare. They learned a lot, they took their lumps, they made mistakes, they fixed the mistakes, and they developed Naval Aviation into what it is today.

While flying from ships remains a dangerous business, it is no longer nearly as dangerous as in the years before World War II.

Sky King!

As a bit of humor, I once posed the question of Rin-Tin-Tin and Lassie knowing one another. By the time I finished writing at the end of the piece, I realized the true answer to the question would determine the age of the reader. If you are a Baby-Boomer, you know Rin-Tin-Tin and Lassie; if you were born after 1970, maybe not.

The *Adventures of Rin-Tin-Tin, The Whirlybirds, Ripcord, Lassie*, and *Sky King* were a few of the television series available to young kids in the late 1950s and early 1960s. The early aviation television shows influenced more young girls and boys into aviation than anyone might realize.

Rin-Tin-Tin and Lassie were just good dog stories and who could say no to watching a television show about dogs? The aviation shows, however, sparked many a baby boomer's imagination, especially those of us living in the shadows of Mercury, Gemini, and Apollo.

Sky King told the story of an Arizona rancher who used his airplane to help others. In the beginning, Schuyler "Sky" King flew an old Cessna T-50, which was later upgraded the Cessna 310B. Occasionally, he would allow his niece Penny to fly the *Songbird*. In the show, she was an accomplished pilot in her own right, holding a multi-engine rating with experience as an air race pilot.

Kirby Grant played the part of Sky King, a former Naval Aviator from World War II. Grant was born on November 24, 1911 and had a very interesting background. As a young child, he leaned toward a musical career as an accomplished violinist. His film career actually began with a bit part as the unaccredited violinist in the musical comedy-romance, "I Dream Too Much." He would later go on to become a full-fledged actor as well as a pilot. The technical representative from Cessna aircraft later commented that Grant flew the 310B as well as any professional pilot.

After the Sky King series ended, Grant retired from both the big screen and little. He moved from California to Florida in the 1970s with his wife, Carolyn. He and Carolyn had visions of creating a nonprofit organization called the Sky King Youth Ranches of America. The organization was to provide for abandoned and orphaned children. Unfortunately, the Grants were unable to realize this dream before his death.

In recognition of his contributions to aviation, NASA invited Grant to the Kennedy Space Center where the astronauts of the Space Shuttle *Challenger* were to honor him for his work in promoting aviation. The mission was STS-16-A, which launched on October 30, 1985. This was the ninth mission of the Shuttle Challenger, the last full mission before the disaster of January 28, 1986.

On the way to the Kennedy Space Center, Grant died in a car accident on Florida's Beeline Expressway near Titusville. He was 73.

Gloria Winters, his co-star who played the part of Penny, died at 77 in Vista, California on August 14, 2010.

The Doolittle Raiders

On the morning of April 18, 1942, 80 very brave men in 16 B-25 *Mitchell* bombers launched from the deck of the aircraft carrier, *USS Hornet*. They and their leaders planned the mission well, but as they steamed toward their targets, they came across a Japanese picket ship.

They did not know if the picket ship compromised their position, even after sinking it. They had to make a quick decision; go now, or wait, and fly the mission as planned. If they took off in the morning, they would lose the cover of darkness. They were almost 200 nm away from their planned departure point, 10 hours early. This meant each of the 16 Army bombers would begin the mission short of fuel.

As the leadership mulled over their decision, they asked questions regarding the success of the mission. Could they do it, or would it fail with the early launch. They also considered the problems of the Chinese in unoccupied China who were to help guide the airplanes to a safe landing and refueling.

There was much to consider and in the end, Doolittle and his Navy counterparts decided it was time to go.

The ship's speakers blared the command, "All Army personnel, man your planes!" As the Army pilots, navigators, bombardiers, and gunners prepared to fly, Navy deck hands walked among the 16 Mitchell bombers passing out additional gas in 5-gallon cans. Still, it would be close.

The crews fired up their planes and got ready. As the commander and leader of the others, Doolittle would be the first off the ship. Placed at the lead meant having the shortest deck run to get airborne. Remember, this was in the days before steam catapults;

these airplanes were going to fly off the carrier into the natural wind over the deck on their own power. If Doolittle could not make it, more than likely, the others would fail also.

As the *Hornet* turned directly into the wind and Doolittle revved his engines, all the crews in the planes behind him stopped breathing for a moment. All eyes were on their leader. Doolittle released his brakes and started his takeoff roll.

His bomber was in the air well before he reached the end of the deck. To the cheers of the other Army pilots and the Navy crews, America was now on her way to return the favor of Pearl Harbor to the Japanese homeland. As Doolittle circled overhead to align his navigation equipment with the direction of the ship, the other bombers continued launching into the sky. They, too, circled overhead aligning their equipment and then headed to their destinations: industrial targets in Tokyo, Kobe, Yokahama, Nagoya, and Osaka. The transit to the Japanese mainland would become routine with very little resistance along the way. The Japanese truly believed they were safe on their island and they had no need to worry about an attack from anywhere.

Lt Col James H. Doolittle leads his men to Tokyo

As they flew to Japan, the bombers stayed low over the Pacific Ocean. The plan called for the pilots to maintain a low altitude to a point just before their targets. At that point, they would sharply climb to a minimal safe altitude for weapons release.

Each bomber carried only four 500-pound bombs along with a full complement of rounds for the machine guns. The bombs were a mix of general-purpose (GP) bombs and high incendiary explosive (HEI) bombs. The intent was to hit the military targets with the GP and spread fires through the region with the HEI.

All of the *Mitchells* hit their targets and escaped to the west. Not one aircraft was lost over the targets. Indeed, only one suffered minor combat damage while over the mainland. It was almost a milk run. Or so it would seem, as they headed to their destinations in China.

The original plan called for the airplanes to leave the ship in the afternoon, which would put them over their targets late at night. They were to fly on to China to arrive at their escape airfields in the first light of morning. With the early detection of the fleet prompting takeoff before they had planned, now they would arrive late in the evening.

Fifteen of the bombers made it to China. One turned north, the pilot concerned for fuel. He landed in Vladivostok, Russia. All 15 airplanes that went to China crashed in the dark of night. The aircraft that landed in Russia was confiscated and the crew interred until their escape in 1943.

Many of the Raiders suffered injury during their crash landings and bailouts, some seriously. Doolittle was one of the lucky ones; he was not injured. One of the more gripping photographs of the famous aviator shows him sitting on the wing of his crashed B-25. Of the photograph, he has said while sitting on the wing of his airplane, he believed he would go home from the war and face courts-martial for the failure of the mission and the loss of so many airplanes and men.

He was so very wrong.

Doolittle won the Medal of Honor for his role in developing the mission, choosing and training the men, and leading them on the

Left to right. Lt. Henry A. Potter, navigator;
Lt. Col. James H. Doolittle, pilot; SSgt. Fred A. Braemer,
bombardier; Lt. Richard E. Cole, copilot; and
SSgt. Paul J. Leonard, fl ight engineer/gunner.

mission. Also for his actions during their escape from the Japanese in occupied territories of China.

Eventually Doolittle attained the rank of general and during the latter part of World War II, he commanded the Eighth Air Force in England.

More Books About Flying

After writing about books on the subject of the Doolittle Raid, I began thinking of other books written about flying every serious pilot should read. There are so many great novels and historical accounts written of flying that once started, are very difficult to put down until finished. There are also great books from which a pilot can learn a lot about flying.

It really is the choice of the reader/pilot. As noted, there are many great stories and wonderful texts. Each allows novice aviators to learn more about flying; as long as the young pilot reads, he or she will learn a lot about airplanes, flight and more.

West with the Night (North Point Press, 1982, ISBN-13: 978-0865471184, 320 pp.) by Beryl Markham is a wonderful firsthand account of learning how to fly in British East Africa, now known as Kenya. Markham was born in England, but moved to British East Africa at a very young age with her mother and father. When her mother decided to return to England, she stayed in Africa with her father.

She lived a very unconventional life and was adventuresome from the beginning, all the way to the end, of her life. Some of the highlights of her life include being the first female in Kenya to drive a car, learn to fly, and then fly across the Atlantic Ocean from west to the east.

She was, in a word, colorful.

When I read her book, *West with the Night,* I was on cruise (as in six-month cruise with the Navy instead of what you're thinking, a three-day gaming and eating festival). A friend had loaned me the book and I tried reading it before leaving for destinations unknown.

When I first started reading the book, I had a difficult time reading beyond the first 20 or so pages. The beginning of the book was…well…slow. So, it sat in the reading box until I had read just about all the other books. Then one day, I picked up the book and read the back cover, something I had not previously done.

The writer wrote about how Beryl lived her life in Africa and went on to say in the most glowing way that she was one of the most talented writers he had ever read. I looked at the signature at the bottom of the paragraph. Ernest Hemingway.

Uhmmm… Maybe I should give this book another go, I thought.

I started reading and during the time that passed since I first read the beginning of the book, the first few pages did not improve. I started to think Hemingway was losing credibility.

When I reached the 21st page or so, I could not put the book down.

Hemingway was right; Markham really was a gifted writer. And oh, the things she wrote about while learning to fly in Africa! Since reading her book, I have wanted to go to Africa to fly. The images of Kilimanjaro and the bush over which she flew and so eloquently described with her words, still remains in my mind's eye to this day.

One day, I hope to go there, and fly where she flew.

-30-

I hope you enjoyed this aviation book from BluewaterPress LLC. We have other aviation titles I think you might enjoy. Included in this list are:

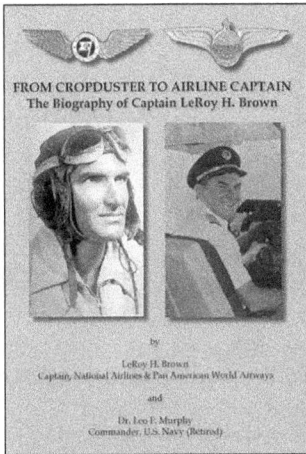

From Cropduster to Airline Captain
By Captain LeRoy H. Brown

This is a fascinating account of how one pilot grew up in Florida, became a cropduster pilot in the 1930s, flew illegally for 400 hours dusting crops, was caught by the CAA, and then talked his way out of a violation and into a commercial pilot certificate. Then he accidently became an airline pilot with National Airlines, and retired out of Pan American Airways at the age of 60 as a DC-10 captain.

LeRoy Brown has penned a fine autobiograpy of his life in the air, but more importantly, his book is a wonderful history of aviation. Written by a pilot who spent his entire life flying, this is a book every serious aviation historian needs to read.

Available online at www.bluewaterpress.com/captain, or through other online retailers and bookstores.

Pan American World Airways - Aviation History in the Words of its People
By JamesBaldwin and Jeff Kriendler

"Pan American World Airways – Aviation History through the Words of its People is a tribute to the legacy of one of the world's great airlines and the men and women who for six decades were the soul of the Company. James Baldwin and Jeff Kriendler have created a compelling book, which through the words of its contributors captures much of the joy, adventure and spirit which was Pan Am."

- *Edward S. Trippe, Chairman, Pan Am Historical Foundation*

Available online at www.bluewaterpress.com, or through other online retailers and bookstores.

Shadow Flight
By Harrison Jones

In *Shadow Flight*, Harrison Jones has spun an aviation tale of kidnapping, drug running, and intrigue. The story opens with flight instructor, Kyle Bennett, teaching slow flight and stalls to one of his students, Brooke Roberts, the wife of a surgeon. Brooke's husband, also a pilot, gave his wife flying lessons as a birthday gift.

Ultimately, that gift could cost both Brooke and her instructor their lives. Fast paced and riveting, this is a flying story that plunges through almost every facet of a flyer's career, from flight instructing to charter work to airline flying. Jones' background as an international captain for a major airline gives him the unique insight required to tell this account of crime and terrorism.

Available online at www.bluewaterpress.com/shadowflight, or through other online retailers and bookstores.

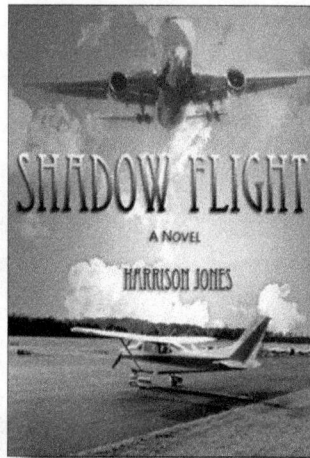

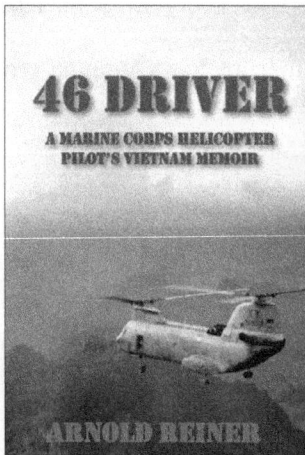

46 Driver
By Arnold Reiner

The kaleidoscopic tale of a Marine Corps CH-46 helicopter pilot and his comrades in Vietnam.

This memoir is a tour through Marine Corps Officer's Candidate School, naval flight training and the quagmire of Vietnam.

Reiner describes landing zones laced with enemy fire, catastrophic inflight mechanical failures, exceptional flying and tragic blunders. It's about life on the drab, hooch-lined bases of Vietnam's coastal plain, Khe Sanh's "hill fights," R&Rs and the crude fleshpots of Da Nang.

But mostly it's about flying and the missions that succeeded and those that did not.

Available online at www.bluewaterpress.com/46driver, or through other online retailers and bookstores.

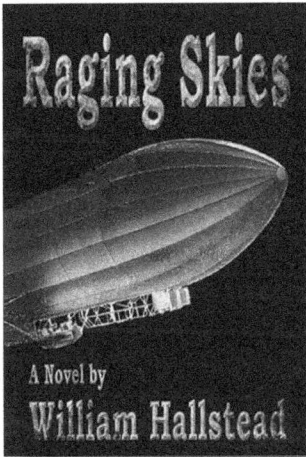

Raging Skies
By William Hallstead

Germany's use of the great Zeppelins in World War I marked the very first time aerial strategic bombing took place in the world. It was a terrible way to wage war. For the British, it was horrible on the ground underneath the behemoths dropping their bombs.

For the Germans flying the great airships, survival became a daily question. Using this historical time as a backdrop, William Hallstead penned a novel of action, adventure, intrigue, love, and espionage.

Konteradmiral Erwin Gunther Kottenhoff is a traditional navy man. He loved the old navy, the battleship navy, his former life on steel decks challenging the restless sea. He detested the way the new airship program deleted national funds he believed should be used in maintaining Germany's first line of defense – the ships he had spent most of his life sailing.

Available online at www.bluewaterpress.com/ragingskies, or through other online retailers and bookstores.

Flying Machines Over Pensacola
By CDR Leo Murphy (USN ret.)

Celebrate the Centennial of powered flight with the achievements of Pensacola's own early aviators!

On December 17, 1903 Orville and Wilbur Wright launched into history with the first powered, controlled and sustained flight of an aeroplane. On November 30, 1911 Pensacola witnessed her own first successful aeroplane flight, beginning with over 90 years of near-continuous aviation achievements and adventures over the Gulf Coast that continues to this day.

Available online at www.bluewaterpress.com/flyingmachines, or through other online retailers and bookstores.

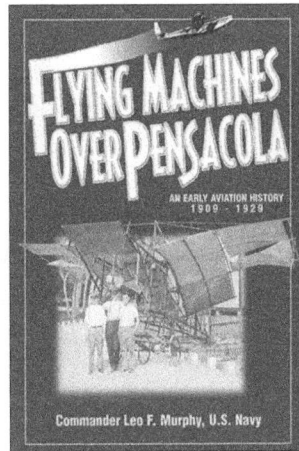

www.ingramcontent.com/pod-product-compliance
Lightning Source LLC
Chambersburg PA
CBHW031250090426
42742CB00007B/397

* 9 7 8 1 6 0 4 5 2 0 7 4 3 *